Women and Political Power
Europe since 1945

Ruth Henig and Simon Henig

London and New York

First published 2001
by Routledge
11 New Fetter Lane, London EC4P 4EE

Simultaneously published in the USA and Canada
by Routledge
29 West 35th Street, New York, NY 10001

Routledge is an imprint of the Taylor & Francis Group

Typeset in Times by BC Typesetting, Bristol
Printed and bound in Great Britain by
Clays Ltd, St Ives, plc

British Library Cataloguing in Publication Data
A catalogue record for this book is available from the British Library

Library of Congress Cataloging in Publication Data
Henig, Ruth B. (Ruth Beatrice)
  Women and political power: Europe since 1945/Ruth Henig and
  Simon Henig.
    p.   cm. – (The making of the contemporary world)
  Includes bibliographical references and index.
  1. Women in politics – Europe. I. Henig, Simon. II. Title. III. Series.

  HQ1236.5.E85 H46 2000
  320′.082′094 – dc21   00-030512

ISBN 0–415–19852–6 (pbk)
ISBN 0–415–19851–8 (hbk)

Women and Political Power

The advance of women through the political system has been one of the most significant developments of the second half of the twentieth century. For the first time we have seen women prime ministers and presidents in Europe.

Women and Political Power examines the extent of progress women have made in ten western European countries, and looks at the factors which have helped, or hindered, their greater involvement in the political process. This book not only explores fascinating contrasts between northern and southern European countries, it also reveals the strong similarities in all countries. It highlights, in particular, the continuing absence of women from leadership positions, and the concentration of women dealing with social and welfare issues.

Women and Political Power is an essential introduction to the experiences of women in politics in Europe since 1945.

Ruth Henig is Dean of Arts and Humanities and Senior Lecturer in History at Lancaster University. Her many books include *Versailles and After* (Routledge, 1995), *Origins of the First World War* (Routledge, 1993) and *Europe, 1870–1945* with Chris Culpin (1997).

Simon Henig is Lecturer in Politics at Sunderland University. He is co-author of *Politico's Guide to the General Election* (2000) and has written on elections in Britain and the political process.

The Making of the Contemporary World
Edited by Eric Evans and Ruth Henig
University of Lancaster

The Making of the Contemporary World series provides challenging interpretations of contemporary issues and debates within strongly defined historical frameworks. The range of the series is global, with each volume drawing together material from a range of disciplines – including economics, politics and sociology. The books in this series present compact, indispensable introductions for students studying the modern world.

Contents

Tables

Acknowledgements

The authors would like to thank all those who helped us to locate relevant sources of information, in particular Claire Price and Diana White in the Enterprise office in Brussels, and Ann-Dorte Christensen and Birte Siim of the Feminist Research Centre at Aalborg University. Work colleagues at Lancaster and at Sunderland were also good sources of advice, and Professor Eric Evans in particular read through the first draft of the book and made many invaluable suggestions. Last but not least our respective spouses as ever provided inspiration and encouragement and did their best to ensure grammatical accuracy. This book is dedicated to the memory of such feminist pioneers as Eleanor Rathbone and Edith Summerskill whose spirited advocacy and tireless campaigning laid the foundations for subsequent progress.

1 Introduction

By 1945, most women in western Europe had won the right to vote and to contest elections on equal terms with men. In some countries, such as Norway and Denmark, political equality had been secured as early as 1907–15; in Sweden, the Netherlands and Britain, female suffrage was conceded at the end of the First World War. The new German Weimar Republic granted women equal political rights with men from the outset, while the short-lived Spanish Republic also gave women political equality, though changes of regime soon reversed the political advances which women in those two countries had made. It was not until the end of the Second World War that German women regained political equality and that French and Italian women were finally able to join with women in most other western European countries in participating in elections on the same terms as men (see Table 1).

But while western European women had finally won their long and hard-fought struggle for political emancipation, the battle to gain a share of real political power was only just beginning, and it was to be a long-drawn-out process. As the leader of the Women's Co-operative Guild noted so perceptively in 1920, two years after women over 30 gained the vote in Britain, 'It is always said that there is equality for men and women in the [Co-operative] movement. Certainly most of the doors are open. But the seats are full and possession is nine-tenths of the law so in reality the opportunity is not equal and seats are hard to win.'[1] Forty years later, Conservative MP Evelyn Emmet echoed the same sentiment, when she commented sharply that men were 'reluctant to see a woman fill any place which might be theirs'.[2]

By 1969, women constituted 15 per cent of the parliament in Sweden, nearly 11 per cent in Denmark and 9 per cent in Norway, yet they had made scarcely any impact in Ireland, with just 2 per cent of seats in the Dáil, in Italy with just under 3 per cent and in Britain with 4 per cent.

Table 1 Dates of first enfranchisement of women and representation in parliament in 1970

	Right to vote	Right to stand as candidates	Parliamentary representation in 1970 (%)
Denmark	1915	1915	10.6
Ireland	1918	1918	2.1
France	1944	1944	1.6
Germany (West)	1918	1918	6.6
Italy	1945	1945	2.8
Netherlands	1919	1917	8.7
Norway	1907	1907	9.3
Sweden	1918	1918	15.5
United Kingdom	1918	1918	4.1

Sources: A. Brill (ed.), *A Rising Public Voice: Women in Politics Worldwide* (New York: The Feminist Press at the City University of New York, 1995); E. Haavio-Mannila *et al.* (eds), *Unfinished Democracy: Women in Nordic Politics* (Oxford: Pergamon, 1985); J. Lovenduski and P. Norris (eds), *Gender and Party Politics* (Sage, 1993).

Note: Figures refer to the lower chamber of Parliament only.

While the participation rates in regional and local government were better than those at national level in some countries, it was emphatically the case, as the United Nations report on the political role of women in Europe noted in 1955, that their influence and power was 'extremely small and grows still smaller as we approach the centre of political leadership'.[3] Twenty years later, the position had scarcely improved. As an American study concluded in 1975, 'An enormous disparity exists between women's formal political equality and their meaningful exercise of political power. Though 99.5% of the women in the world are legally entitled to participate in the political process, the numbers of women in public office remain in most countries appallingly low.'[4]

Since 1980, a steadily increasing output of books and articles by sociologists and political scientists, many of them women, has sought to explain why women have found it so difficult to convert theoretical political equality into real political power. On the one hand, a wealth of institutional, cultural and socio-economic factors have been cited as obstacles to women's progress. They include family and domestic responsibilities, a continuing willingness to accept a traditional role in society, norms of 'good motherhood', reluctance to challenge the influence of the church and its teachings, particularly in Catholic countries, gender stratification at school and a consequent lack of educational qualifications, lower participation rates than men in employment and trade union activities, and the structure of political parties and of electoral systems. On the other hand, from the 1970s, feminist activists and writers have increasingly drawn attention to the nature of political structures and to definitions of the 'political'. They have argued that legislation alone cannot overturn the ideologies and assumptions that continue to underpin male domination. They point out that women have been kept out of politics both by political structures which are perceived as 'oppressive' and by long-standing political conventions that have divided life into 'public' and 'private' spheres. As a popular saying in Sweden in the early twentieth century ran, men should work in the 'large household' while women should confine themselves to the 'small household'.[5] The Dutch Calvinist theologian, Abraham Kuyper, explained in his book, *The Honorary Position of Women*, written in 1914, that God had ordained that 'Woman is not equal to the Man in public life.' He argued that

> There is a double life. A life in the family, with the children, that has a more private aspect. And then there is another life, almost totally divorced from the first, a life of councils and states, of navies and armies, that has a more public character. This double kind of life demands extremely distinct gifts and talents and . . . these double kinds of gifts and talents . . . appear to coincide with the differences in kind between man and woman. Private and public life are two distinct spheres, each with its own way of existence . . .[6]

Thus, while women were granted political equality, enduring political and social conventions combined to keep them out of the political arena. Political agendas, as defined by men, continued, until the 1970s and beyond, to embrace only public issues, leaving concerns such as those relating to family relationships and reproductive rights firmly in the private sphere. Thus, issues of fundamental concern to women, such as fertility rights and divorce rights, were not defined as political issues. Furthermore, women's growing involvement in social welfare work was still regarded as an extension of their domestic role and did not draw them into the formal political arena in great numbers. The few women who did achieve success within traditional political structures were only able to operate effectively in a male world, it was alleged, 'so long as they behave there as men'.[7]

Much change has taken place in the last two decades of the twentieth century in the fields of education, training and employment. Many of the barriers which allegedly held back women's involvement in the political arena, such as lack of educational or professional qualifications or low levels of participation in the workplace, have been removed. Across the European Union, 110 women now have higher education qualifications for every 100 men, and at general upper secondary school level, 124 girls obtain a qualification for every 100 boys. Far more women now work than ever before, albeit often in part-time jobs, and though the employment rates of men up to 1999 were consistently higher than those of women in all European Union member states, the gap was closing fast in Sweden, Finland and in one of the non-EU countries, Norway. Women are also now well represented in initial vocational and training programmes, though again they are outnumbered by men by 55 per cent to 45 per cent.[8]

Yet despite taking advantage of greater educational and employment opportunities, women still find it difficult to access political power at the end of the twentieth century. Research from countries across western Europe reveals that

> women are almost never represented in decision-making positions in proportion to their presence in [an] . . . organisation, that there is extensive male resistance to women's participation in decision making and that the problems of reconciling the competing claims of personal life, working life and civil or public life are everywhere more difficult for women than for men.[9]

What this book seeks to do is to measure the extent and nature of the advance of women into positions of political power in the last 50 or so years, drawing on the experience of ten western European countries. The slogan adopted at the United Nations conference on equality issues held in Beijing in 1995 was 'Half of the world: half of the power'. What distance has still to be travelled by women in western Europe before that objective is realised? Chapter 2 will look at the period from the end of the Second World War to the end of the 1960s to see what kind of obstacles prevented women from moving beyond formal political emancipation, why it proved so difficult for them to secure more than a tenuous hold on political power during this time and whether those rare women who did reach senior government positions shared similar backgrounds or had any characteristics in common. The 1970s was undoubtedly a crucial decade for women throughout western Europe. Hundreds of feminist groups drew inspiration from the United States and from a stream of seminal works focusing on different aspects of women's liberation and began to redefine and to broaden the political agenda; millions of women participated in campaigns to secure the right to abortion, divorce on the same terms as men and equal pay. Chapter 3 will try to explain why women became involved in a wide range of political activities from the early 1970s onwards and will examine the division between those women who argued that women's interests could be served only by working outside formal political structures and those who believed that existing structures could most effectively be changed from within. It will also look at the impact of women's campaigns at local level in terms of widening the political agenda and drawing large numbers of women into feminist activity. Chapter 4 looks at the ways in which and the extent to which political parties in different western European countries responded to the broadening of the political agenda and sought to accommodate the increasing political interest and involvement of women to gain their support. It has been argued that women members of socialist and radical parties have been more successful in gaining parliamentary selection and indeed ministerial power than their counterparts in Christian democrat or conservative parties. Yet at the same time, in nearly all political hierarchies in the countries being studied, women remained heavily concentrated at the lowest levels into the 1980s and were strikingly absent from the higher reaches of power and influence. Chapters 4 and 5 will consider these issues and Chapter 4 will specifically examine the crucial impact of the adoption of quotas for women candidates.

By the mid-1990s, women were steadily increasing their representation at government level, and were taking on a range of ministerial posts. Chapter 5 will assess the impact of women in national politics in terms of the areas of interests they have pursued and the nature of the posts they have been given. Do women still occupy predominantly the 'social' and 'welfare' posts, or are they being assigned other important posts such as economic or foreign policy portfolios? To what extent have women been the victims of 'functional marginalisation'? Are there some posts still seen as more suitable for male incumbents? This chapter will consider these issues, and also the extent to which the few women promoted to leadership positions tried to get more women onto the ministerial ladder. The following chapters will switch attention to two very different arenas in which women were competing for political power, the sub-national and the international. Chapter 6 will examine the extent to which local government has served for women as an entry-point into the wider political arena and the importance of supporting women's networks. It will also consider the validity of the 'iron rule' – that the more powerful the position, the less likely it is to be filled by a women – by assessing the extent to which women have been successful in becoming mayors of major cities or regional and local government leaders. Chapter 7 will consider the growing impact of the European Union both in terms of its evolving legislative framework and community directives to which community members have to adhere, and also in terms of the increasing female membership of the European Parliament and the Commission. It will also look at the influence of United Nations' initiatives and conferences on women's issues.

Many political scientists have argued that the most important factor affecting the numbers of women who are able to exercise power within a political system is the nature of the particular electoral system employed. Specifically, it has been argued that a proportional representation system is a crucial enabling condition for women to break through into a political system in large numbers. Chapter 8 will assess the importance of electoral systems to see how great their impact has been. And finally, after two decades of increased political participation, we should be able to raise such questions as: Has women's involvement in western European political systems made a discernible difference? Do women operate differently to men and do they display distinct political skills and interests? Are women in a number of different western European countries pursuing similar specific agendas? Chapter 9 will assess the evidence drawn from the previous chapters and will begin to frame answers to such questions.

This book aims to build on the existing literature in the field of women's political activity in two ways: first, by synthesising the mass of recent secondary works on women and political power, and second, by drawing on data and publications from ten countries in western Europe. The countries on which this study is based include the five major powers in the European Union: France, Germany, Great Britain, Italy and Spain; three Scandinavian countries: Denmark, Norway and Sweden; and two smaller nations: Ireland and the Netherlands. In some ways these ten countries share important common features; all are prosperous, all are liberal democracies, and all except Norway are members of the European Union. In addition, the geographical distances between the ten countries are significantly less than those between the eastern and western coasts of the United States. For these reasons, then, we might assume a broadly similar pattern in the political progress made by women in the ten countries since the Second World War.

Yet the similarities between the ten countries hide a number of potentially significant variations, including different histories, party systems, political cultures, social and family structures. For example, Great Britain can boast a centuries-old unbroken parliamentary tradition, while France has had five republics since overthrowing the *ancien régime* in the 1789 Revolution. Germany had only an unhappy experience of democracy before the Second World War, with a stable parliamentary democracy not being formed until the 1950s. Spain had to wait until even later before democracy became established, with the first national elections after the fall of Franco taking place in 1977. In terms of party systems, there have been significant differences in the political systems in the ten countries. Until recently, the Swedish and Italian political systems have each been dominated by a single party (the Christian Democrats and Social Democrats respectively). Single-party governments have been the norm in Britain, but in a majority of our other countries coalition governments have been a permanent feature. Most party systems have been dominated by classic left against right party competition, but the Irish party system has remained distinct, and that in the Netherlands more divided than in most of the other countries in the group. In addition, some countries have maintained very centralised structures of power, while others (such as Spain and Germany) have become more decentralised, with significant power being devolved to regional or local bodies.

Culturally, there are major differences between Scandinavia/ northern Europe and countries in southern Europe such as Italy and Spain. In particular, it has often been argued that the relatively 'open' political culture in Scandinavian countries has facilitated women's access to power, whereas 'closed' political cultures elsewhere have acted to prevent such progress. In four countries, France, Italy, Spain and Ireland, the Catholic church has traditionally exercised a powerful influence on politics and society, whereas it has been argued that in northern Europe the (Protestant) church has now lost any political influence it may have once enjoyed. It has also sometimes been argued that Britain has closer cultural ties with the United States than with mainland Europe, facilitated by a common language. For geographical reasons, the Nordic countries may also have developed in different ways to the European mainland, and it may be significant that Sweden did not join the European Union until 1995, and that in a referendum Norway voted to remain outside.

Some or all of these factors may therefore have led to important differences between the ten countries included in this book. The many variations provide a context within which the progress of women into positions of political power in each country can be viewed. It is more difficult of course to judge whether the successful experiences of women in some individual countries can be repeated elsewhere, in different political and social environments. For example, have the Scandinavian countries blazed a trail which women across western Europe can follow, or are there aspects of Scandinavian political, economic and/or social structures which are unique to northern Europe, and which could not be successfully exported to southern Europe?

EXISTING LITERATURE AND DATA

One of the problems of researching this book has been the unevenness of the material available, and the relative absence of detailed studies of women's pursuit and exercise of political power. While the women's studies sections of academic libraries are full of books which examine the sociological, cultural and psychological aspects of gender issues, there is comparatively little on women's political behaviour or on women as political leaders. The handful of senior women politicians who have written their memoirs or who have been the subjects of major biographies do not enable us very easily to draw comparisons or gain insights into why they were so successful and in what ways they challenged existing political conventions. Thus far, there are few studies based on the experiences of significant numbers of women politicians at national or local level covering the factors which first drew them into political activity, their views on the operation of political organisations or their strategies for exercising power.[10]

We have drawn heavily on some definitive studies, such as *Women in European Politics* (Lovenduski 1986), *Gender and Party Politics* (Lovenduski and Norris 1993) and *Women in Politics: An International Perspective* (Randall 1982). Other useful books included *Women and Government: New Ways to Political Power* (Kelber 1994), *Women and Politics Worldwide* (Nelson and Chowdhury 1994) and two books primarily focusing on Scandinavia: *Unfinished Democracy: Women in Nordic Politics* (Haavio-Mannila *et al.* 1985) and *Women in Nordic Politics: Closing the gap* (Karvonen and Selle 1995). We have also found compilation volumes, based on conference papers, such as *The New Women's Movement* (Dahlerup 1986), *The Women's Movements of the United States and Western Europe* (Katzenstein and Mueller 1987) and *Women and Politics in Western Europe* (Bashevkin 1985) extremely useful in their detailed analyses. The publications of the European Commission, especially from the Employment and Social Affairs Directorate covering equal opportunities issues, have provided invaluable data and trends on recent developments across EU countries, as have the reports of the Expert Network on Women in Decision Making. Recent reports issued by bodies such as the Council of European Municipalities and Regions *(Men and Women in European Municipalities* and *Women's Participation in Political Life in the Regions of Europe)* and the EU Committee of the Regions (*Regional and Local Democracy in the European Union*) have also provided much valuable information.

None the less, the published material on the extent of women's participation in western European politics and the power they are able to wield at the end of the twentieth century is still not voluminous and remains uneven in coverage. For example, little has been written about women within bureaucracies, whether within governments or political parties. Likewise, there is a surprising absence of major studies on women in the trade unions or in non-governmental organisations or on the women's movements of the 1970s. One of the most serious gaps relates to the extent of influence wielded by religious bodies and specifically by the Catholic church on women's social and political behaviour and on political culture in general. As a result, these areas have been to a large extent ignored in this volume, not because they are unimportant areas of study, but because of the absence of available literature. However, we have attempted to bring together the disparate data which exists on the influence of the European Union and on women in local government, areas which are often missing from studies of women and power. One of the main purposes of writing this book is to encourage further research and publication both on the topics covered and perhaps even more importantly on those issues which we have omitted through lack of information.

2 Slow progress, 1945–1970

While most adult women in western Europe were able to vote and to participate fully in public life from 1945, relatively few succeeded in becoming representatives at either national or local level in the following 25 years. This chapter looks at some of the reasons which have been suggested for this painfully slow progress, and also at some of the underlying factors which in the longer term laid the foundations for change. We shall start by looking at the impact of the Second World War, at prevailing social and economic attitudes in the 1950s and at the provisions of the new constitutions that were adopted in Germany, France and Italy immediately after the war. We shall then consider the extent to which women voted disproportionately for right-wing parties in this period, yet paradoxically were more likely to be adopted as candidates by parties of the left. In his classic study, *The Political Role of Women*, published in 1955, the French political scientist Maurice Duverger claimed that women showed significantly less interest in politics than men. We clearly need to consider the extent to which, and the reasons why, this was the case. None the less, by the end of the period, we shall find women campaigning actively in a number of countries for equal pay and for laws to legalise birth control and abortion. To what extent were these campaigns led by female members of parliament, and how great was the influence women representatives wielded at government level by the end of 1960s?

THE IMPACT OF THE SECOND WORLD WAR

Fierce debates still continue amongst historians about both the overall impact of the two twentieth-century world wars and more specifically about their effect on the role and status of women in society. At one extreme, the wars are seen as watersheds, fatally undermining the prevailing social and political order and bringing fundamental and last-ing changes to the lives of millions. At the other extreme, historians stress underlying continuities and lengthy, slow patterns of economic and social change which are barely interrupted by the wars.[1]

There can be no question that both world wars, and particularly the second, had a major impact on the lives of both single and married women. In Britain, nearly half a million women joined the armed forces and over 80,000 became members of the Women's Land Army; 7.75 million women worked and another million 'did their bit' in the Women's Voluntary Service. In Germany, the Nazi regime was adamant that a woman's place was in the home, producing the Aryan heroes of the future and providing for her family. In spite of a desperate labour shortage by 1943 and pleas from those responsible for the war effort, Hitler repeatedly refused to conscript women into the labour force. As a result, there was only a tiny increase in the numbers of women employed during the war. None the less, it is clear from Gestapo records and from oral testimony that the lives even of the majority of women classified as 'Aryan' were greatly affected by the racial policies pursued by the Third Reich and by the increasing privations of war.[2] And for the few Jewish women, in Germany and across occupied Europe, who survived the war, life could never be the same again.

Across occupied Europe, and particularly in France, Italy and the Netherlands, women played key roles in resistance movements. They kept family farms and businesses going and moved into jobs hitherto regarded as exclusively male preserves in shipbuilding, vehicle building, metalwork, chemicals and engineering works. While war work was initially seen as a necessary and perhaps unwelcome contribution to the national war effort, it inevitably had the effect of widening hori-zons, drawing women into new and more permissive social networks and enabling them to develop self-confidence and a sense of self-worth. A British nursemaid who became a steel worker recalled how the experience 'made me stand on my own feet, gave me more self-confidence', and a women's voluntary service worker in Barrow confided to her diary in 1942, 'I wondered if people would *ever* go back to the old ways. I cannot see women settling to trivial ways – women who have done worthwhile things.'[3]

The Second World War was indeed a 'People's War' – and women found themselves in many different and often dangerous situations on the front line, and relished the experience. A British government social survey in 1943 revealed that most women who had jobs during the war were reluctant to give them up when the war ended. The main answer given to the question, 'What do you value most about war work?' was inevitably 'the money', but 'the company' was not far behind. In 1945, the economist Gertrude Williams observed, 'War has shown how many women welcomed employment as a relief from the monotony and isolation of domestic work. The gossip of the shop, the companionship of fellow workers, the opportunity to see new faces and make new friends are all sources of pleasure.'[4]

On the other hand, it is possible to exaggerate the impact of the war. The numbers of women in civilian employment in Britain only rose from 4.8 million to 6.7 million between 1939 and 1943. And 85 per cent of women who were working during the war were already in paid employment when it started. Nearly 10 million women in Britain declared themselves 'unavailable' for work, even part time work. Those who did move into the work-force found themselves working for less money than the men who had been doing the job before them. And there was a clear expectation, underlined by wartime agreements between the government and the unions, that after the war was over, the men returning from war service would step back into their pre-war jobs and the women who had temporarily filled them would return home.[5] Even in the immediate post-war years in occupied Germany, where an acute labour shortage led to the general conscription of women into paid work in 1946, their role was clearly temporary without any permanent prospects, and as men became available they were quickly replaced.[6]

Statistics on female participation rates in the labour force reinforce this view of the war as having little immediate impact. In Britain, the percentage of women working fell from 34.2 per cent in 1931 to 32.7 per cent in 1951.[7] In Germany, female employment in 1950 was at its lowest level since the First World War.[8] Indeed, in both these countries, it is argued, there was a retreat by women back into the domestic sphere as a result of the experiences of the war. There was an understandable longing to concentrate on the restoration of family life, to return to pre-war normality and to a stable domestic routine after the dislocation caused by the war. In this sense the war could be said to have been a retrogressive experience, reinforcing women's traditional domestic roles and responsibilities. Indeed, the celebrated Beveridge reforms, which were hailed as one of the greatest achievements arising from the war and which heralded the birth of the welfare state in Britain were implicitly based on a male breadwinner model, in which a woman's role was seen as being dependent on her husband. As Pamela Graves has noted, male Liberal economists provided the models:

Labour men debated them and the mostly male Members of Parliament gave them the force of law. Excluded from their party's decision-making process, Labour women had no opportunity to contribute from their considerable knowledge and experience of social welfare reform to their party's postwar policies.[9]

Thus, while the war clearly brought considerable changes to women's lives, these were often short-lived. Entrenched attitudes regarding a woman's role in society as primarily centred on home and family persisted after the war. None the less, in the longer term, women had demonstrated their abilities and had begun to explore a world beyond the domestic sphere. As we saw in Chapter 1, they were also politically enfranchised in France and Italy, and re-enfranchised in Germany. While it was to take nearly three decades for the 'unspoken social assumptions' of the immediate post-war period to be seriously challenged, there can be no doubt that women's experiences during the war had a long-term impact.

WOMEN AND POLITICS AFTER 1945

What political impact did the war have on women? We have already noted that women played an important role in European resistance movements and this, together with the strong influence of the American political model, is reflected in the new constitutions which were drafted at the end of the war in France, Italy and Germany. In France, the preamble to the constitution of the Fourth Republic granted women equal civil, economic and political rights. Similarly, in Italy, equality between the sexes was written into the new republican constitution. Article 3 of the new West German constitution explicitly stated that men and women were to enjoy equal rights and that no one was to be prejudiced or privileged because of their sex. It is interesting to contrast these constitutions, drafted immediately after the war, with the last European constitution of the inter-war period, the constitution of Ireland, which dates from 1937. Ireland shared with France and Italy a strong Catholicism, yet the provisions of its constitution were far more restrictive for women, possibly revealing the extent to which the experiences of the war subsequently helped to change attitudes. One of the clauses of the Irish constitution banned divorce and there was also a ban on married women working in the civil service, local government or for health boards. Furthermore, Article 41 emphasised that home duties were more important than labour.[10]

Yet did these post-war equality clauses in France, Germany and Italy have any practical result? Not only was there little subsequent legislation to put them into effect, but prejudices against women working or becoming involved in political activity remained strong. Nearly twenty years later, in 1965, 72 per cent of men and 68 per cent of women in West Germany thought it was 'not normal' for married women to work, and as late as 1975 a majority of men said that politics should be left to men.[11] The belief that a working wife reflected badly on her husband, by revealing his inability to support her, remained strong in the two decades after the war.

How actively did women wish to become involved in politics in this period? Studies from the inter-war period suggest a considerable amount of interest amongst women in Britain to secure social reforms, better maternity services, family allowances and the right to practise birth control. Women had served on school boards in England and Wales since 1870, and they also played a prominent role in inter-war peace campaigns.[12] In Norway, there were already twenty 'women's unions' at the turn of the century. Between the wars, concerted campaigns were launched to get women onto boards of education, child welfare committees and poor relief boards and to become involved in local politics.[13] In France in the 1930s women had campaigned vigorously for the vote. However, it has been argued that the immediate post-war years were 'a more difficult period for women's political participation' in France, once full political equality had been granted.[14]

It has been suggested that one important reason for the lack of women's involvement in politics in the immediate post-war period was that women were uninterested in politics. As part of his United Nations study into the political role of women carried out in the early 1950s, Maurice Duverger found that in France only 13 per cent of women declared themselves to be interested in politics as against 60 per cent who were not. Only 35 per cent of women discussed political topics compared with 70 per cent of men. There was also a clear belief that politics was a 'male world'.[15] In West Germany, the turnout of German women in elections in the 1950s was lower than that of men, and 'the majority of the women showed little interest in politics'.[16] As late as 1977, while 66 per cent of West German men declared themselves to be interested in politics, only 33 per cent of West German women expressed themselves in similar terms.[17] And in Italy, through to the 1970s, women accepted that politics was 'a man's affair'.[18] However, as feminists in recent years have emphasised, the definition of 'politics' in this period remained very male-orientated, still reflecting the origins of the word which dated back to the period of the Greek city-state, when 'political' activity was discourse and decision-making carried out in public by citizens (all male) as opposed to private, domestic household activity. Thus, it excluded issues deemed to be personal and to belong to the domestic sphere, such as fertility rights and family matters which were of interest to women. Hardly surprisingly, therefore, women saw less reason to become politically active and to vote than men. In addition, most women had onerous domestic responsibilities which in some cases they combined with part-time or full-time employment, leaving them very little time for political activity even if they had wanted to become involved. Furthermore, they had not by and large benefited from the same educational opportunities as men.

A handful of women were elected to national parliaments in 1945, however. In France and Italy, where women were able to stand for election for the first time, they constituted nearly 7 per cent of the new French National Assembly and nearly 8 per cent of the Italian Chamber of Deputies. However, these totals were boosted by a large number of female communist deputies, possibly reflecting their politicisation in the wartime resistance movements, and in subsequent elections the numbers of women in parliament dropped in both countries (see Table 2). What is striking about the overall 1945 data is the uniformly low number of women elected and the absence of significant variations between countries – just over 4 per cent separated the leaders, Sweden and Italy, from Ireland, which had the lowest percentage. By 1970, however, a considerable gap had opened up between the three Nordic countries, which moved into double figure percentage representation, and Ireland, France and Italy, with derisory levels below 3 per cent.

One possible explanation for the higher numbers of women elected in Scandinavia is that parties of the left have been more ready to place women candidates in positions where they can be elected. Between 1945 and 1970, in every general election, there were more women elected from the British Labour Party, Norwegian Labour Party and Swedish Social Democrats than from all other parties in those countries put together. When one adds to that the dominant position in Sweden of the Social Democrats since the 1930s, this goes a long way towards explaining the steady increase in Swedish female representation by 1970. However, in Italy and France the left found itself in permanent opposition from the late 1940s, and the numbers of female communist deputies fell quite sharply, helping to explain the very low levels of women's representation by 1970.

One of the most interesting features of women's political behaviour during this period is that across a number of countries they were more

Table 2 Women in parliament in 1945 and 1970

	% Parliamentary representation in 1945*	% Parliamentary representation 1970	% Change 1945–70
Denmark	5.4	10.6	+5.2
Ireland	3.4	2.1	−1.3
France	6.9	1.6	−5.3
Germany (West)	6.8	6.6	−0.2
Italy	7.8	2.8	−5.0
Norway	4.7	9.3	+4.6
Sweden	7.8	15.5	+7.7
United Kingdom	3.8	4.1	+0.3

Sources: E. Haavio-Mannila *et al.* (eds), *Unfinished Democracy: Women in Nordic Politics* (Oxford: Pergamon, 1985); J. Lovenduski and P. Norris (eds), *Gender and Party Politics* (London: Sage, 1993); S. Donnelly, *Elections '97* (Dublin: Seán Donnelly, 1998).

Note: Figures refer to the lower chamber of parliament only.

* The figures given in the second column of the table refer to the number of women elected to the lower chamber of parliament at the first election held after the end of the Second World War. In the case of the UK and Scandinavian countries this was 1945, but the first post-war general election in Ireland was not held until 1948, while the first full parliamentary elections in the new Italian Republic and Federal Republic of West Germany took place in 1948 and 1949, respectively.

likely to support parties of the right, even though such parties traditionally adopted few women candidates. In West Germany, the Christian Democrats (CDU) and their Bavarian sister party (the CSU) attracted 10 per cent more votes from women than from men in the 1950s and 1960s. Support amongst women for the Social Democratic party was low.[19] In Britain, the Conservatives secured approximately five per cent more votes from women than from men in this period, and indeed it has even been suggested, somewhat speculatively, that 'if Britain had continued with an exclusively male franchise, all other things being equal, there could have been an unbroken period of Labour governments from 1945 to 1979'.[20] There were also significant 'gender gaps' in both France and Italy in this period, with women traditionally voting for right-wing parties.

A number of explanations have been put forward to account for this pattern of political behaviour. In Italy, women's preference for the Christian Democrats has been linked to the traditional support of women for the Catholic church and its organisations. In France, too, Catholicism has been seen as an essential element explaining women's voting habits, with women attending church more frequently than men. However, in Britain, it is often argued that the influence of religion on voting behaviour has been minimal throughout the twentieth century, so we need to look elsewhere for an explanation of women's support for the Conservative Party. One possible hypothesis is that the Labour Party and associated trade unions in Britain have been perceived as heavily male-dominated. A second explanation is that women were more inclined to vote for parties which represented 'stability' and 'respectability', which has been argued to apply also in West Germany. Whatever the explanation, it is interesting to note that the right–left 'gender gap' had disappeared in many of these countries by the end of the 1970s.

WOMEN IN NATIONAL POLITICS

Though relatively few in overall numbers, some women did manage to break through into national politics by the end of the 1960s and make a significant impact. Did they share any characteristics in common? And did they raise gender issues and make common cause with women in other political parties, or advance their careers by 'putting party loyalty before their principles', a charge levelled against Labour women MPs by Britain's first woman MP, Lady Astor, at a Suffragette Fellowship meeting in 1950?[21]

If one tries to draw general conclusions mainly from British examples about the factors which helped women to establish national political careers, some interesting points emerge. A careful choice of family background was important, preferably one with middle-class professional parents, but even more helpful was a family with 'strong political connections or a record of public service'.[22] It seems that fathers played a particularly crucial role in encouraging their daughters to develop an interest in politics rather than confine themselves to domestic matters. By treating their precocious offspring as surrogate sons, they instilled self-confidence and a sense that almost any professional activity or career might be pursued. As Margaret Thatcher recalled in her autobiography, each week her father took two books out of the library, 'a "serious" book for himself (and me) and a novel for my mother'.[23] Jennie Lee enjoyed a similarly close relationship with her father, and was brought up as 'the son of the family'.[24]

Nearly all British women MPs elected from the 1930s to the 1960s completed their secondary education; many then proceeded to women's colleges at Oxford or Cambridge or to London or other big city universities. Data from the Netherlands confirms that women representatives in this period came largely from upper-middle-class families and completed a university degree before becoming lawyers or teachers.[25] In Britain, would-be candidates first took up professional careers as teachers, doctors, journalists or in industry, and often gained local government experience before embarking on the hazardous quest of finding a winnable or safe parliamentary seat. A handful of MPs, like Margaret Bondfield and Ellen Wilkinson in the inter-war period, received encouragement and sponsorship from a trade union, but this was relatively unusual. For the most part, women had to battle against male scepticism and female hostility on local selection committees to gain adoption as candidates. For married women, this could be a daunting prospect; indeed, in the Netherlands up to the Second World War, married women with children were regarded as unacceptable candidates, especially by the religious parties.[26] Even in post-war Britain, would-be candidates needed great reserves of confidence, persistence and faith in their own abilities. Margaret Thatcher, having fought a creditable campaign for the Conservatives in an unwinnable seat in 1950, was rejected by some safe constituencies in the later 1950s, on the grounds that she had two young children and would find it impossible to combine a parliamentary career with her family responsibilities. She later recalled that some women on local selection committees had expressed the view that the House of Commons 'was not a suitable place for women with children'.[27] As *The Times'* political correspondent commented in 1962, when trying to explain why there had only been 76 women MPs in Britain in 43 years, it was 'still a man's world for women politicians . . . on any view the women politicians have all the big cards stacked against them when they take the high road to Westminster and so it will continue'.[28] The eminent playwright, George Bernard Shaw, acknowledging the problems women faced, put forward a novel solution in a letter of support to the Labour candidate for Flint, Eirene Jones (later Eirene White) in 1950. He advocated the 'coupled' vote to get more women into parliament, whereby each elector 'had to vote for a man and a woman' or the vote would be invalid.[29]

Once elected to Parliament, women soon discovered that the House of Commons was, in Margaret Thatcher's words, a very 'masculine' place, particularly because of the 'sheer volume of noise'. To Edith Summerskill, in the late 1930s, 'Parliament, with its conventions and protocol, seemed a little like a boy's school which had decided to take a few girls.'[30] The result was a considerable amount of taunting and of sexist behaviour. Serious arguments about access to family planning or about inequalities in pay were parried by comments about clothes and appearance. Thus, when, in 1941, Edith Summerskill pointed out in a House of Commons debate that even Ernest Bevin admitted 'my figures [on pay inequalities between men and women] are right', Bevin retorted, 'I think your figure's perfect.'[31]

To be successful, and to make their mark in such a male-dominated environment, women had to compete with men on their terms and be tough. The *New Statesman* in 1966 attributed Barbara Castle's success to the fact that she had 'always accepted the business of politics on men's terms, attacking hard and expecting no quarter'. Another cabinet minister under Harold Wilson, Jennie Lee, once said that she had never made a speech 'speaking as a woman' in her life. As her biographer comments, 'she did not identify with women' and 'had never led a gendered life'.[32] But Labour women MPs also subordinated gender issues to those of class, which they regarded as far more important. While they frequently spoke on health, housing and education matters, they argued that social improvements for women would come only as a result of the eradication of class inequalities. Thus, the battle for women's rights was only a subordinate part of the main battle for socialism, and it was this latter battle which principally consumed the energies of Barbara Castle, Jennie Lee, Eirene White, Peggy Herbison, Judith Hart and other women ministers who served in Harold Wilson's 1964–70 Labour governments. Similarly, Conservative ministers of the 1950s and early 1960s, such as Pat Hornsby-Smith, Mervyn Pike and Margaret Thatcher pursued the political agenda drawn up by the party's male members. Revealingly, Thatcher commented that her role in Edward Heath's shadow cabinet in the later 1960s was 'as the statutory woman whose main task was to explain what women . . . were likely to think and want on troublesome issues' though we should be careful about taking her comments at face value.[33]

None the less, there were issues of specific concern to women which women MPs pursued or on which they co-operated across party lines. Barbara Castle led a celebrated and successful campaign in the early 1960s to abolish the penny charge which women had to pay at the turnstile entrance of most municipal women's toilets. Some women MPs pressed for the right for married women to be taxed separately from their husbands. Margaret Thatcher and Eirene White gave a joint press conference in the summer of 1961 about the lack of provision for the needs of pre-school children in the new high-rise flats which were being built throughout the country. Eirene White also battled hard for improved benefits for widows, and Bessie Braddock fought for the housewives of Liverpool. But when it came to issues of fundamental importance to all women, such as equal pay, family limitation or abortion, only two women MPs put gender interests above all others and saw themselves as feminists first and foremost, Eleanor Rathbone, an independent representative of the Universities, and Labour's Edith Summerskill.

Edith Summerskill, a married doctor practising under her maiden name, unsuccessfully contested a by-election in Bury in 1935 in which, in the face of strong opposition from the churches, she campaigned on the right of women to be allowed to practise birth control. She was elected in West Fulham in 1938 and began to campaign to extend the right of wives to matrimonial property and to ease their financial dependence on their husbands. Having served as a junior minister in the 1945–50 Labour government, she turned her attention in the 1950s to the campaign to secure equal pay for women. While by this time there was no longer any bar on married women working, female wages lagged well behind those of male colleagues, even if they were doing the same job. Though the principle of equal pay for women in public sector employment was included in the election manifestos of all the major parties in 1950, it was not until 1954 that the Conservative government agreed to the gradual introduction of equal pay in the civil service, and until 1955 for the introduction of equal pay in the teaching profession. The principle was then extended to the NHS and to the gas and electricity industries, but not to private sector businesses.

Whilst Edith Summerskill campaigned tirelessly for equal pay in the 1950s, it fell to Barbara Castle, appointed by Harold Wilson as secretary of state for employment in the late 1960s, to pilot through Parliament the Equal Pay Act of 1970, giving employers five years to ensure that equal pay would be granted to women doing the same jobs as men. Similarly in Norway and Sweden, in the 1950s, campaigns for equal pay were mounted by female parliamentary representatives, leading to the Swedish government signing the United Nations convention on equal pay in 1960. In Norway, the establishment of an Equal Pay Council in 1959 was followed by the widespread implementation of equal pay across private and public sector employment between 1961 and 1967. But in other western European countries, though the Treaty of Rome establishing the European Economic Community stipulated in article 119 that men and women should receive equal pay, little concrete action followed until the 1970s.

The other issues on which women representatives in some countries made progress in the late 1950s and 1960s were divorce and abortion. In Germany, divorce became more accessible after 1958, and in Italy it became possible in the late 1960s. Sweden established advice centres on contraception in the 1960s and in France contraception was legalised for adult married women in 1967. Abortion was legalised in Norway in 1960, and in Britain, female pressure helped to secure the passing of David Steel's Abortion Law reform bill in 1967 and was even more significant in subsequent years in working with a broad range of interest groups to prevent any restrictive amendments to the legislation.

Whilst it was not until the late 1960s, as we shall see in the next chapter, that women became involved in such issues in great numbers, the few women who did establish themselves as politicians at national level found increasing opportunities to exercise influence over a wide range of policies. Whereas in Britain in 1957 the *Daily Telegraph* (19 January) commented that 'Education, Health and Pensions are the Ministries thought most suitable for women Under-Secretaries', reflecting what was thought to be their 'natural' interest in family and welfare issues, by the end of the 1960s a considerable change had taken place. In Harold Wilson's 1966 government, Eirene White created something of a stir when she was appointed to a ministerial position in the Foreign Office. Jennie Lee was appointed Minister for the Arts, and was given the task of drafting the legislation to establish the 'University of the Air', and thence to get the Open University, as it became known, up and running. Judith Hart became a Minister of State at the Commonwealth Relations Office, and Barbara Castle was the Secretary of State for Transport before taking over Employment. For the first time Labour women were appointed to the Whips' Office, though it was to take another 30 years for the Conservatives to follow suit. None the less, on the Conservative front bench in the late 1960s, Margaret Thatcher became the spokesperson for Treasury and Economic Affairs. In Sweden, one of the architects of the Swedish welfare state in the 1930s, Alva Myrdal, who had been appointed to head the United Nations Department of Social Affairs in 1949, finally became a member of the Swedish cabinet in 1967 at the age of nearly 65, with the post of minister of disarmament. Her husband had been a cabinet minister 25 years previously, but as she commented, he had really preceeded her by only four years, since she had to add on 20 years 'for the handicap of being a woman'.[34] In the Netherlands, in 1956, Marga Klompe, who had served in the Dutch resistance during the war, became the first female cabinet minister and served altogether in five cabinets, though no other women were appointed at this level until the late 1970s.

Thus, by the end of the 1960s a few determined, confident, committed women were playing major roles in national politics. Once in national legislatures, because they were relatively few in number and because they had already had to prove their abilities in the hard battles to get selected, they found it comparatively easy to catch the eye of senior party figures and to gain promotion up the ministerial ladder. But there were still many obstacles standing between aspiring female politicians and a full-time career in national politics. The political playing field was by no means level between the sexes and, as we shall see, while increasing numbers of women in the 1970s struggled hard to change the situation from within existing political structures, others argued that women could only become truly emancipated if they worked through women-only networks.

3   Second wave feminism
The 1970s and early 1980s

The movement which has become known as 'second wave feminism' emerged in several western European countries in the late 1960s. Whereas the first wave of feminist activity was principally concerned with gaining the right to vote, by the 1960s it was clear that women were still socially and politically disadvantaged. Thus, the term 'second wave feminism' covers a whole variety of disparate organisations, groups and campaigns seeking to liberate women from what were perceived to be oppressive male structures and to promote genuine equality between the sexes.[1] There has been much discussion about the reasons why so many women became involved in women's protest movements at this particular time. Clearly, the activism and feminist writings of women in the United States in the early and mid-1960s inspired many women in Europe.[2] At the same time, peace campaigns like the Campaign for Nuclear Disarmament (CND) movement in Britain and the student protest movements of the later 1960s in many west European countries drew growing numbers of women into political activism. By the mid-1960s, women had increasing access to further and higher education. Alongside growing educational opportunities, the mass marketing of labour-saving devices reduced the amount of time which needed to be spent on housework, and the growing availability of contraceptives enabled women to control their fertility and to limit family size. Furthermore, the 1960s was a time of economic growth in western Europe, and increasing numbers of women, both married and single, were drawn into employment. However, as more opportunities opened up for women, they became more aware of the discrimination they faced in the workplace and of the contradictions between the emancipated role outside the home that they were increasingly able to play and the traditional expectations which still defined a women's place in society.

As we shall see, second wave feminism contained many diverse strands, and took different forms from country to country. In its ambitious aim to transform society, it encompassed a range of agendas including economic issues, sexual concerns, family issues, the use of language and interpretations of history. As a result of its campaigns, and their impact in reformulating the political agenda, it had a major impact throughout western Europe, being described by the Danish feminist Drude Dahlerup as 'one of the most important social movements of the post-war period'.[3] By raising new issues and causing old ones to be redefined and by influencing public opinion, women's activities in the 1970s significantly broadened the political agenda. They were also successful in bringing into existence a growing feminist consciousness. This chapter will first discuss the various strands of second wave feminism and assess what the many different women's groups aimed to achieve, and will then examine its specific impact in our ten European countries. By the 1970s, women were becoming prominent in new forms of political campaigning linking environmental concerns with anti-nuclear protests, and were increasingly active in informal local networks. The chapter will assess these developments and the distinctive contribution they have made in broadening political agendas by the end of the 1970s.

CATEGORIES OF FEMINIST GROUPS

It has been argued that the women's movements of the late 1960s and 1970s 'typically consist[ed] of two branches', an older branch of liberal or moderate groups aiming to achieve equal rights for women within the existing social system, and a younger, more radical and ideologically motivated branch wanting to transform society in accordance with feminist principles.[4] 'Equal rights', 'liberal' or 'welfare' feminism was particularly strong in Sweden and Norway, and was also influential in Denmark and in Holland. Very different in its aims and objectives was 'radical' or 'socialist' feminism, which argued that working through existing political structures would merely serve to perpetuate the oppression of women. Rooted in the New Left protest movements of the late 1960s, radical and socialist feminists campaigned to break down the male domination of society and to work for the liberation of all oppressed people, particularly women. While socialist feminists placed the blame for the exploitation and oppression of women on class as well as gender, radical feminists emphasised sex as the fundamental division in society. Socialist and radical feminists ran particularly effective campaigns in Italy and Spain, and were also prominent in France, Denmark and Britain, though acrimonious debates between the two groups and with liberal feminists in the 1970s increasingly undermined their effectiveness.

While 'women's rights' groups campaigned to secure equality for women by exerting pressure on existing political structures, more radical feminists argued that women had to create new political structures and a new political discourse. Arguing that domestic issues hitherto regarded as personal such as child-rearing, housework, marriage and love were in fact issues loaded with profound political significance, their claim 'the personal is political', which was inspired by earlier feminist and civil rights campaigners in the United States, challenged and greatly expanded traditional definitions of what should be regarded as 'political'. Furthermore, they pointed out that broader conceptions of what could be regarded as legitimate political activity, which were not confined to conventional political frameworks, included the self-help projects, networking and co-operative ventures in which women had always been active at local level.

Thus, one aim of the more radical feminist groups in the 1970s was to draw public attention to the continuing oppression of women by men through high-profile activities. An example in August, 1970, was the attempt by nine French radical feminists to lay a wreath to the wife of the Unknown Soldier in the Arc de Triomphe in Paris, on which was inscribed 'there is one about whom even less is known than the Unknown Soldier: his wife'. Four months earlier in Copenhagen, a group of about 15 Danish women marched down the main pedestrian area

> audaciously and grotesquely dressed, caricaturing the com-
> mercialised image of women as stupid sex object. On their route
> they shouted feminist slogans . . . At the main square . . . they
> took off all their artificial female attributes – bras, roll-ons,
> artificial eyelashes and wigs – and threw them into a wastebasket
> on which was written 'Keep Denmark tidy'.[5]

A second aim was to construct new political frameworks through which women could work to achieve their goals, free from male domination. Not only was it argued that women's approaches to political activity were very different to those of men, seeking to work through loose networks in a flexible way rather than to construct hierarchical structures, but that their concerns were also seen to be more practical and immediate, centring on health issues, the provision of day care centres and safe refuges and on environmental problems. Thus, the 1970s saw the emergence of well-women centres, rape crisis centres and safe women's refuges all staffed and run by women.

But the most significant aim was to challenge the traditional view that such issues as contraception, abortion and divorce were not mainstream political concerns. These issues were in fact highly political, argued feminists, and were a striking illustration of the continuing way in which men oppressed women and defined the political agenda to ensure their dominance. Only women should be given the responsibility and the right to control their own fertility. Thus, free abortion on demand became one of the central goals of feminist groups throughout western Europe, and the principal battle ground on which they waged their struggles against male-dominated political parties and governments.

As we shall see, significant changes in legislation relating to such issues as abortion and divorce took place in the 1970s across western Europe. These resulted from the efforts of feminist activists, although the new laws were frequently more limited than women campaigners had demanded. In countries such as Norway and Sweden where such legislation was already more favourable to women than elsewhere, campaigns centred instead on equality issues. We shall consider the activities in these two countries first, then turn to Denmark and Holland, and then look at Italy, Spain and France, before turning to Britain, West Germany and Ireland.

SWEDEN AND NORWAY

In Sweden, women's sections had developed since the turn of the century 'in virtually every party, union, professional, social and religious organisation in the nation'.[6] The result was that 'reformist' feminism had become a strong force influencing the political agenda, especially of the Social Democratic Party which had dominated Swedish government since the 1930s. Early in the 1960s, a woman journalist, Eva Moberg, wrote a pamphlet entitled 'The Conditional Emancipation of Women' which 'sparked a national "sex role" debate' by questioning why, just because women gave birth to children, they should also assume, in addition to childcare duties, all the washing, cooking and domestic chores.[7] The result was that by the end of the decade the Swedish government explicitly adopted the goal of a society based on independent individuals and began to formulate an official sex equality policy to recognise this. A number of measures followed, including provision for the separate taxation of married couples, the right of all to work, and the establishment in 1976 of a parliamentary committee on equality. The implementation of a 'parents' insurance' programme enabled fathers as well as mothers to stay home during the first year of a child's life, and working mothers were assisted by the provision of new day care centres. In 1980, an ombudsman for equality was appointed.

Perhaps it was hardly surprising, therefore, that there was little radical feminist activity in Sweden in the 1970s. Legislation regarding reproductive rights were in advance of other European countries: laws prohibiting abortion were first reformed in 1938 and from the 1950s contraceptive advice centres were available to all women over the age of 15. In 1975, an abortion act was passed which enabled women to have abortions on demand and provided a full range of supportive public services. Subsequently rape within marriage was recognised as a criminal offence.[8] Thus women's groups and organisations within Sweden achieved considerable success in reaching their goals by working within existing political structures, which perhaps explains the relative weakness and ineffectiveness of the few radical feminist groups which were formed there in the late 1960s.

In Norway, while new feminist groups emerged in the late 1960s and 1970s aiming to 'transform structures along feminist principles', they were willing to work alongside established women's organisations on a range of issues including demands for a more liberal abortion law, secured in 1978, and for equal pay.[9] Quite soon, strong links formed between the different women's groups, as they all worked together across party, class and ideological lines to explain the workings of the electoral system to women voters and to campaign for the election of as many women as possible both at local and at national level. As in Sweden, the goal in the early 1970s was to secure equal opportunities for and equal treatment of women. Thus, in 1972 the Equal Status Council was established, which replaced the Equal Pay Council which had existed since 1959. However, radical feminist groups argued strongly that women needed additional help to enable them to compete on equal terms with men, otherwise the pursuit of equality would simply lead to the 'assimilation of women into the male-created and dominated public realm on unequal terms'.[10] They stressed the fact that women's approaches to politics were different from those of men, and that formal political structures needed to reflect female, as well as male, political cultures. The result in 1978 was the adoption by the

Norwegian parliament of the legally ground-breaking Equal Status Act which, while it promoted equality between the sexes, aimed particularly to improve the position of women by giving them special rights on account of their sex. The Act recognised that, because only women experienced pregnancy and childbirth, their situation was different from that of men. Positive discrimination was required to enable them to secure real equality. Thus, strong campaigning and close collaboration between a range of different women's groups and organisations laid the foundations in the 1970s for a dramatic transformation of the Norwegian social and political system over the following 20 years.

DENMARK AND THE NETHERLANDS

In these two countries, radical feminist groups emerged in the 1970s to challenge existing social and political structures and to campaign for liberation for women. At the same time, long-established 'women's rights' groups were exerting pressure within the political system to secure greater equality for women, and the interaction of these different approaches resulted in the adoption of many important new measures in both countries.

A number of loosely organised, diffuse feminist groups of mainly young and middle-class women emerged in Denmark at the beginning of 1970, from the New Left and student movements. They were inspired by the example of female activists in the United States and Britain, and wanted to challenge both the existing Danish patriarchal social structure and the older women's groups who, they alleged, had not fought strongly enough to overturn it. They used direct action to get across their message, operating under the banner of the 'Redstockings', a name they borrowed from the New York Redstockings. Two examples of their tactics help to explain why they quickly attracted the attention of the Danish media:

> On Mother's Day [May 1970, in Copenhagen] a group of women entered a public bus and refused to pay more than 80% of the fare because women get only 80% of the salary of men. They were – peacefully – arrested and fined, but they refused to pay more than 80% of the penalty . . . During a beauty contest [in summer 1971, in Aarhus] a group of Redstockings interrupted the event, conducted by a popular TV host, and protested against

the exploitation of women as sex objects and women competing for the benefit of men only.[11]

The radical feminist movement spread from Copenhagen to other Danish cities and set up Women's Houses to act as meeting points for feminist activists. A feminist festival was held in Copenhagen in 1974, which attracted 30,000 visitors to listen to the speeches and enjoy the music of all-women bands. It became the first of many such events. At the same time, radical feminists campaigned with other groups to demand free abortion and equal pay. In 1973, a liberal abortion act which had been passed in 1970 was replaced by a Termination of Pregnancy Act which provided for free abortion on demand during the first 12 weeks of pregnancy. It was followed in 1974 by the Social Assistance Act which established a wide network of day care and recreation centres for children and young people subsidised by public municipal funds. And the 1976 Equal Pay Act provided for equal pay for equal work.[12]

At the same time, the older-established women's groups and women in parliament were continuing their efforts to secure greater social and workplace equality for women. The Commission on the Status of Women in Society, which had operated in the 1960s and early 1970s, was replaced in 1975 by the Equal Status Council whose task was to work to eliminate inequality 'in the hiring, training, promotion and working conditions of women and men' and to 'oversee affirmative action in the public sector and education'. The Council became statutory three years later with the passing of the Equal Treatment Act which specified equal treatment of men and women in employment, education and other areas.[13] Subsequently, in each county an 'equality consultant' was appointed to enable women to improve their position in the labour market and to break down sex segregation. A symbolic but important change in the marriage law was passed in 1984, whereby a woman would keep her own family name on marriage unless she explicitly chose to take the name of her new husband; a reciprocal provision was available to men. Radical feminist groups were scathing about such attempts to transform the existing social structure rather than to overturn it completely, yet there is no doubt that the combination of 'the indirect impact of the new movement through its renewal of the feminist debate and the direct effect of actions by feminists working inside the political institutions' to secure equal status brought about considerable social and economic changes which greatly benefited women.[14]

There were striking similarities between events in Denmark and in the Netherlands. Radical feminist groups emerged in the Netherlands in the late 1960s out of student protest campaigns and quickly attracted national attention. In particular, the 'Dolle Mina' group, arising out of student and left-wing politics, built up a wide following and organised many consciousness-raising events which were fully covered by the Dutch media. By 1982, it was estimated that there were nearly 160 feminist groups, covering a quarter of all Dutch towns.[15] Radical feminists focused their activities strongly at grassroots level, campaigning to establish rape crisis centres, women's health groups and adult education centres to encourage women returners. But their greatest achievement was in redefining the abortion issue as a women's issue whereas hitherto it had been seen as a 'medical or psychological problem'.[16] Though the new Abortion Bill of 1981, which came into force in 1984, was paradoxically somewhat less liberal than the existing system in practice (because the previous law had become widely discredited), women's groups had succeeded in forcing change on unwilling political parties and had mounted a successful challenge to the way in which issues like abortion were perceived by Dutch politicians.

At the same time, long-established women's groups, some operating in women's wings of political parties and in trade unions, worked to increase the numbers of female political representatives. The Dutch Association for Women's Interests sought to mobilise voters to vote for women candidates and put pressure on parties to nominate more women candidates. A major objective was to speed up the achievement of social equality between the sexes, and in 1974 the Emancipation Commission was set up as an independent advisory body to help the government to formulate a coherent policy for the emancipation of women. In 1977 a state secretary was appointed to co-ordinate and to promote an emancipation policy, supervised by a special Emancipation Council, and a year later a state sub-department was established for the 'Co-ordination of Equality Policy' in addition to a special parliamentary committee on emancipation policy. Government subsidies were made available to help projects which promoted women's emancipation, and 'femocrats', activists from the women's movement, were recruited into government departments to give advice and assistance with the establishment of such projects at local level. Once again, as in Denmark, despite the misgivings of some radical activists, the parallel efforts of radical feminist groups and of older more traditional women's organisations had proved very successful in helping to establish in the Netherlands 'the most extensive and comprehensive [sex equality apparatus] in Europe'.[17]

ITALY, SPAIN AND FRANCE

In terms of attitudes towards the social and economic emancipation of women, these three Catholic countries were not as advanced in the late 1960s as the four northern European countries we have just considered. Outside the major urban areas, a strong Catholic church worked closely with traditional local and regional networks to emphasise the family responsibilities and domestic roles of women. However, the 1960s was a decade of economic expansion and of widening educational opportunities which laid the foundations for change. In all three countries, new feminist groups became active in the 1970s and pressed strongly for divorce law and abortion reforms and for greater economic equality.

In France, feminist activity grew out of the student protests of May 1968. Over a hundred feminist groups, some of them very small, ranging from revolutionary and radical groups to those advocating syndicalist, socialist or reformist approaches, emerged in the following two years.[18] Though many of the groups have been described as rather intellectual and elitist in approach, sometimes aloof, largely Paris-dominated and often bitterly opposed to each other,[19] they were able to join forces effectively in a campaign to secure a more liberal abortion law. Contraception had been legalised in France in 1967 and this opened the way for a campaign to repeal a law of 1920 which banned contraception and abortion. As in the Netherlands, French feminist groups argued that control of fertility should be solely a woman's responsibility and that she should have the right to decide whether or not to have an abortion. The forces of opposition – centred on the Catholic church, the parties of the right and conservative doctors – were strong, and feminist activists therefore sought national publicity to demonstrate that considerable numbers of women who could afford to secure abortions elsewhere were flouting the existing laws. They also tried to encourage more women to seek abortions. Their aim was to force the government to take action against those who were openly flouting the law, thus forcing confrontation over how socially divisive and ineffective the existing ban on abortion actually was.[20]

Feminist groups worked with representatives of trade unions and of centre-left political parties in the early 1970s to bring pressure to bear on the French parliament to reform the abortion law. Finally, after heated debate in the French Assembly, accompanied by a vigorous media-led public discussion, abortion during the first 12 weeks of pregnancy was legalised in 1975. The legislation was originally to operate for five years but in 1979 the reform was made permanent. Also in 1975, an important series of laws was passed to forbid sex discrimination at work, to give equivalent rights to mothers as to fathers with regard to running domestic affairs, and to give wives the same rights as husbands in relation to the matrimonial home. At the same time the divorce laws were reformed so that the consequences of male and female adultery were legally identical. Subsequent legislation redefined rape and the penalties for it.

Political parties were not slow to respond to the new mood of militancy amongst French women. In December 1972, a statute was passed which accepted that there should be equal pay for equal work. Two years later, a State Secretariat for Women's Condition was established, and in 1978 this became a delegated ministry. And in 1981, a Women's Ministry was established under Yvette Roudy, which oversaw the enactment of a framework of laws to lay down a programme of equality in employment for women. It has been claimed that during the 1970s the French women's movement changed 'the universe of political discourse'.[21] Rejecting traditional norms, 'feminists put forward a radical concept of gender relations in sexuality, emotional and economic independence, formal and real equality in marriage, the family and other existing relations of sexist domination'.[22] It is undoubtedly the case that by the early 1980s some significant legislative changes had taken place. French governments now placed greater emphasis on issues affecting women and were prepared to give them a higher legislative priority than would have been the case a decade earlier.

The Italian feminist movement, as in France, emerged from the radical student movement of the late 1960s and quickly found itself in conflict with the Catholic church and with the dominant Christian Democrat Party over issues such as divorce reform, abortion and the removal of church influence from education. As in France, the movement was strongest in such major urban and industrial centres as Rome, Milan and Turin, where it could draw support from long-established political and cultural traditions of radicalism. In the early 1970s feminist activists worked through hundreds of consciousness-raising autonomous women's groups such as Rivolta Femminile (Female Revolt), the Collettivo Femminista Romano (Roman Feminist Collective) and Lotta Femminista (Feminist Struggle). Such groups were keen to stress that they were part of an evolving movement which was not in any way connected to the existing political structure, that they excluded men, and were egalitarian and participative in approach rather than hierarchical.[23] Inevitably, however, they were viewed suspiciously by local Communist and Socialist Party organisations whose agendas were dominated by economic issues and not by social concerns which could potentially weaken the unity of the working class. In the early 1970s, the Italian Communist Party castigated feminists as 'petty bourgeois' and 'individualistic' and argued that Italy was 'not ready' to confront women's issues.[24] However, feminist struggles to liberate Italian women attracted increasing support. One important area of success was the establishment of medical centres to treat working-class women, which helped to forge links between feminist activists and the local community in cities like Turin. Up to two million Italian women became involved in feminist campaigning,[25] and many of the new recruits, especially amongst younger women, were keen to form alliances with existing political and professional organisations or to work within them. Despite such differences in approach, the Italian feminist movement as a whole was particularly successful in enlisting support for legislative change from trade unions and even, ultimately, from the largest opposition party, the Communist Party, and has been described as 'the largest, most vital and successful' women's movement in Europe.[26]

In 1970, the Italian parliament approved a divorce law which allowed for civil divorce after a five-year separation. The Catholic church immediately began to campaign to overturn it, and looked to its traditional areas of support, including large numbers of women in rural and semi-rural areas, to back a referendum to reverse the legislation. However, when the referendum was held, in 1974, nearly 60 per cent of the population voted against any change to the new law, despite the fact that 68 per cent of women and 53 per cent of men had been against its introduction in 1970.[27] Though women's groups had supported the campaign to maintain the new law, they had viewed it as a fight in support of civil rights and democracy rather than for women's rights. Now the outcome of the referendum suggested that further reform favouring women's interests was a real possibility.

According to Italy's 1931 penal code, abortion was punishable by imprisonment. By the late 1960s, it was estimated that between one and three million Italian women per year were securing illegal abortions, despite the fact that the code was still operative.[28] In response to feminist activity in the early 1970s, a campaign began to collect the half million signatures required to bring about a referendum to legalise abortion, and in 1973 a Socialist deputy introduced a Bill into the Chamber of Deputies to achieve the same goal. As the Catholic church and its allies tried increasingly desperately to hold back reform, feminist activists working with their allies in the trade unions and in the political parties of the left mobilised ever-bigger public demonstrations in favour of change. In 1975, two mass protests attracted first 10,000 and, later in the year, 30,000 supporters, and in the 1976 national elections, pressure from women's groups contributed to significant electoral gains by the parties of the left. As the Chamber of Deputies debated a measure that would allow abortion but with doctors, rather than women themselves, being given the power to take a final decision, 50,000 protesters took to the streets. Finally, in 1978, a new abortion law was passed which represented a compromise between feminist activists' demands for a woman's right to choose and the opposition to abortion of the Catholic church. Women over 18 could in future obtain abortions up to 90 days after conception in public hospitals on medical, social or economic grounds, but doctors and health staff were allowed to refuse to carry out abortions on grounds of conscience. This concession was immediately invoked by large numbers of medical staff and had a serious impact, particularly in southern Italy, where it remained difficult for women to secure abortions, despite the new law. Whilst feminists felt that the reform fell far short of what they had demanded, pro-life groups were appalled at the new provision, and organised a referendum to overturn it. However, the percentage of those voting to maintain the abortion law was even higher than the level of support for divorce reform in 1974. Of those who took part in the referendum, held in 1981, 67.9 per cent supported the legalisation of abortion. But attempts by Italian feminists to petition the Chamber of Deputies to pass a law prohibiting and redefining violence against women, an area of particular concern, especially in southern Italy, were not successful in mobilising enough political support for the measure.

None the less, another significant change had taken place in 1973, when the advertising and use of contraceptives in Italy was finally permitted. Two years later a new family law was approved which asserted the equality of marriage partners and of their responsibilities in relation to the education of their children. And in 1977, in order to bring Italian law into line with European Community law, an Equal Pay Act and Equal Opportunities Act were introduced. Thus, by the end of the 1970s, the pressure exerted by feminist campaigns had helped to bring about considerable political and social change in a country in which women had not hitherto played a very active political role. Women's groups had successfully challenged the power of the Catholic church and the preconceptions of the predominantly male Italian deputies and had placed women's issues firmly on the Italian political agenda.

In Spain, the strong position of the Catholic church under the dictatorship of General Franco, which lasted until his death in 1975, greatly restricted women's social and economic freedoms. Divorce, contraception and abortion were all illegal and adultery was severely punished. Wives were expected to obey their husbands, to concern themselves with family and domestic chores and with religious observance, and not to work outside the home. However, the development of the Spanish economy and particularly of the tourist industry in the 1960s helped to create a more open society and to promote social and cultural liberalisation. The educational and employment opportunities available to women had begun to increase substantially by the late 1960s, and a number of women began to join in left-wing political activity aimed at the ending of dictatorship in Spain. However, it was not until the mid-1970s that a feminist movement as such took shape.

As in other European countries, feminist activists divided into radical, socialist and equal rights groups and debated the merits of separatist organisation and activity as against working through established political organisations. But they united in pressing for the legalisation of divorce, contraception and abortion, and for the end of discrimination in education and employment. Franco's death in 1975, which coincided with the proclamation by the United Nations of 1975 as International Women's Year, gave a boost to the new women's movement which was further encouraged by the emergence of democracy in Spain. A new constitution, established in 1978, prohibited discrimination on grounds of sex and proclaimed equal rights for men and women. In the same year, the ban on information about, and sale of, contraceptives was removed, and a network of health centres was established to provide guidance on family problems. Civil divorce became possible in 1982, and two years later abortions were legalised, although, as in Italy, doctors could refuse to carry them out on moral grounds. Because abortions could only take place if the mother's life was in danger, the foetus was malformed, or the woman was a rape victim, feminists objected that the measure was far too restrictive and furthermore that abortion was not to be provided free by the state. None the less, the measure represented a significant advance which had been partly brought about by pressure from women's groups, though the growing strength of the Socialist Party in the National Assembly was arguably a more important factor. By 1985, it is estimated that there were more than 600 women's groups in Spain, but many of them were very small, and only about a fifth were explicitly feminist.[29] Nevertheless, many different strands of feminism were active in the ten years after Franco's death, both in the major cities and at regional level, and helped to contribute to the significant changes in the social and political climate which took place.

BRITAIN AND WEST GERMANY

There are many similarities between the feminist movements which developed in the late 1960s in Britain and West Germany. Both drew inspiration from contemporary developments in the United States and emerged out of the student protest movements of the late 1960s. In both countries, the agenda was set by radical or socialist feminists rather than by liberal or reformist groups. And both movements had much greater success in stimulating local campaigns and promoting political change at local level than they had in influencing the national agenda.

In Britain, a broad range of radical and socialist women's groups was active in the 1970s, but they remained relatively small in membership and rarely co-ordinated their campaigns. They have been described as a 'deliberately dispersed collection of groups, campaigns and political structures with no single ideology'.[30] In 1983 it was estimated that about 10,000 women were active in some 300 groups, with a further 20,000 active on the periphery, but such numbers were very modest compared to the three million women in 1978 who met regularly in Britain to pursue a wide range of activities through such organisations as the Women's Institutes, Townswomen's Guilds, WRVS and the Mother's Union, but who did not for the most part regard themselves as feminists or see themselves as participating in a 'combative engagement' with male supremacy.

The four main demands of feminist activists in the 1970s were free contraception, equal pay, educational and job opportunities, the availability of 24-hour nurseries and abortion on demand. The 1967 Abortion Act had legalised abortion on a number of specified grounds up to 28 weeks, and while feminists were unsuccessful in their campaigns to broaden the scope of the legislation, they were able to mobilise mass support and draw on considerable trade union strength through the establishment in 1975 of the National Abortion Campaign which co-ordinated the efforts of some 400 separate groups and organisations. Thus, in 1975 and again in1979 they were able to prevent two attempts by backbench MPs to restrict the provisions of the 1967 Act.[31] While free contraception and adequate childcare facilities were not achieved in the short term, the Labour administration which came to power in 1974 introduced a Sex Discrimination Act in 1975, followed by the Employment Protection Act, which gave women a statutory right to paid maternity leave, protection from unfair dismissal during pregnancy and the right to regain jobs up to 29 weeks after giving birth. The establishment of an Equal Opportunities Commission also held out some hope for women of a move towards equal pay and equal opportunities in future years.

Feminist activists were most successful in initiating political and social change at a local level. Activists highlighted the extent and trauma of rape and of domestic violence suffered by women, and in 1972 the women's aid movement was established by Erin Pizzey. By the end of the 1970s, 99 women's aid groups and 200 women's refuges had been set up. One concrete result of this activity was the introduction of the Domestic Violence Act in 1976, whereby women could get a court injunction to restrain a violent husband or partner. By 1981, 16 rape crisis centres had also been established, partly as a result of pressure on local councils being successfully mobilised by individual women's groups.[32] Another encouraging development in the later 1970s was the establishment of women's health centres, which offered a range of practical advice, help and counselling services.

Feminist activists tried hard to highlight women's continuing oppression at the hands of men, and also the virtual absence of women below the rank of royalty from history textbooks. One result was the establishment of a number of publishing collectives, and the launching of the periodical *Spare Rib* in 1972, which helped to maintain the momentum of the feminist movement. Another was the establishment of women's studies workshops and the emergence of women's studies as an academic programme in a growing number of universities and polytechnics. All this helped in the longer term to promote and to spread understanding of the feminist perspective. Also significant for the longer term, in its strategy to work from within rather than to work through self-sufficient networks, was the establishment of the 300 Group, which aimed to increase to just under 50 per cent the number of women in the House of Commons, and which had recruited some 3,000 female members by 1982.

In Germany, a strong women's movement emerged in West Berlin in the late 1960s and quickly spread to other major German cities. Radical feminist groups flourished in West German universities and focused on grassroots activism. Vigorous local campaigning helped to establish rape crisis centres, battered wives' shelters and publishing co-operatives, but feminists found it far more difficult to make an impact at national level. One of their earliest and most important aims was to bring into being a new abortion law which would provide for abortion on demand. Though a more liberal measure was agreed by the Bundestag in 1975, it fell well short of feminist demands. Nevertheless, pressure from a broad coalition of women's groups and organisations had helped to bring about at least some change.

In 1973 the Bundestag established a Women and Society Commission to look into the status of German women, and numerous measures were suggested by its subsequent report. But concrete changes promoting equality were slow to be implemented, and a law providing for equality for women in the labour market was introduced only as a result of EEC initiatives. Between 1980 and 1990, hundreds of equality counsellors were introduced into regional and local councils and then in the civil service, political parties, universities and trade unions, though their powers to promote change were somewhat limited. As in Britain, while feminist activists were successful in promoting awareness of the range of problems faced by women in a local context, they found it difficult to bring pressure to bear on the government or on political parties to introduce major change into their national political agendas.

IRELAND

Ireland provided the most hostile environment for feminists in the 1970s. As in other strongly Catholic countries, divorce and abortion were then illegal and the sale of contraceptives prohibited. Though some women's groups were established in the late 1960s and 1970s in Dublin and other major cities, their activities were greeted with horror and outrage. Demands for contraceptive services and for equal pay, and campaigns for the establishment of rape crisis centres and women's refuges met with considerable opposition. It was not until 1979 that a family planning law legalised contraception for married couples, and only in 1985 could single people over the age of 18 buy contraceptives legally. The bans on divorce and on abortion remained in force, and in the early 1980s pro-life groups sought to strengthen the law against abortion by bestowing on the foetus the right to life. In a referendum held on the issue in 1983, two-thirds of those voting supported the change in the law, and only a third voted against. As far as the status of women was concerned, Ireland undoubtedly lagged well behind the other nine countries at the end of the 1970s.

ANTI-NUCLEAR AND PEACE CAMPAIGNING AND
THE GREEN MOVEMENT

As women became increasingly active in feminist campaigning and in redefining the political agenda in the 1970s, they became particularly identified with two political developments, the spread across western Europe of anti-nuclear protests, culminating in campaigning against the introduction by NATO of American cruise missiles, and the emergence of 'eco-feminism'. For many decades women in a number of European countries had participated actively in peace campaigns. One example was the veteran British campaigner Dora Russell who had fought for a number of women's causes in the inter-war period but confessed that 'for me, the struggle of the women's movement for peace was first on the agenda'.[33] But peace campaigning had rarely engaged large numbers, though it should be noted that in the sizeable CND marches and campaigns of the late 1950s and early 1960s in Britain, women activists outnumbered men by two to one.

As the Cold War reached its climax in the early 1970s with the continuing threat of nuclear war, protests against nuclear power and against nuclear weapons spread, sometimes helped by feminist campaigning. In 1974, demonstrations against the use of nuclear power started in Denmark and spread to Germany and the Netherlands. A major nuclear alarm at a generating station in the United States in 1979, in which a serious radioactive accident was narrowly averted, sparked off two enormous protests in Denmark. The realisation of the damage which could be caused, particularly to women and to their unborn children, by exposure to high levels of radiation brought large numbers of women on to the streets to join in anti-nuclear demonstrations. In the summer of 1981, thousands of European women, organised by five Norwegian women's peace groups, marched to Brussels in protest against the nuclear arms race. And in a referendum in Sweden about nuclear power in March 1980, 46 per cent of women but only 31 per cent of men opposed its use.[34]

In Britain, in the summer of 1981, press reports about the Norwegian women's march to Brussels prompted the organisation of a similar march, with a women's 'core group' and female organisation and leadership, from Cardiff to Greenham, where NATO Cruise missiles were to be sited. Forty walkers – 36 women and four men, plus three children – completed the 110-mile journey to the US base in Berkshire, and when the media failed to cover the event, four women chained themselves to the fence of the base. The marchers established a peace camp, and from February 1982 it became a women-only camp, attracting not only widespread media publicity but inspiring similar camps to be established at Molesworth in Cambridgeshire, Upper Heyford in Oxfordshire and Faslane on the Clyde in Scotland. Attempts to evict the women and to prosecute breaches of the peace led to high-profile court cases and to increased support for the women of the Greenham peace camp. As a result of a campaign to 'embrace the base', about 30,000 women descended on Newbury, surrounded the base, clasped hands and pinned mementoes on the perimeter fence. A women's International Day for Disarmament in June 1983 was marked by no fewer than 600 local demonstrations and events. And, in political terms, all this campaigning seemed to be having an impact on at least half of the electorate. The *Sunday Times* noted that the Tory lead over Labour amongst women voters in 1983 had fallen from 10 per cent to 2 per cent, 'and the indication is that disarmament is the issue that has influenced this shift'.[35]

In other European countries where cruise and Pershing missiles were due to be installed, campaigns were mounted and peace camps were set up. In West Germany, Italy, Belgium and the Netherlands, women took a prominent part in the demonstrations, and began to forge links with environmental and anti-poverty action groups. One campaigner who achieved international media recognition in the early 1980s was a European civil servant, Petra Kelly, who, as part of her work for the EU's Economic and Social Committee, had researched the connections between sexual discrimination, poverty, environmental degradation and nuclear policy, and who left the West German Social Democratic Party (SPD) in 1979 over the decision to station cruise and Pershing II missiles on European and particularly German soil. Avowedly feminist by the late 1970s, she condemned Europe in 1975 as 'one big male supremacy bastion – the church, the political parties, the trade unions, the national bureaucracies, the European Institutions'. By the early 1980s she was fighting for 'feminism, ecology and non-violence' and was developing the concept of 'eco-feminism'.[36] She played a major role in building the West German Green Party into a powerful electoral force, with a strong complement of women candidates, and in the 1987 Bundestag elections, the Green Party received over three million votes and gained 44 seats, 25 of them occupied by women. For the first time in the history of the German Bundestag, a party group had a majority of women members.

CONCLUSION

Thus, by the early 1980s, feminist campaigners had not only challenged the political agenda within individual west European countries but had introduced new and imaginative approaches to political activism. They had asserted that while women felt oppressed by male-dominated political structures, and took little part in them, this did not signal a lack of interest in political issues as such but rather concealed a fundamental difference of view about what issues should be regarded as 'political'. Millions of women throughout western Europe participated in campaigns to liberalise divorce and abortion laws, went on peace marches and became involved in environmental campaigns. As a result, they became increasingly involved in the political process while at the same time they developed new approaches to campaigning and effective ways of networking.

At the same time, the more flamboyant and explicitly feminist protests undoubtedly provoked a backlash. Female campaigning was met with derision and criticised as being too strident, reminiscent of the general reaction to the campaigns of suffragettes in the first wave of feminist activity in the early twentieth century. Large demonstrations of women demanding the right to obtain divorce and abortion were seen by many older and conservative groups in society throughout western Europe, particularly in rural areas, as threatening and deeply destabilising. Such activities provoked a spirited response particularly from the Catholic church, and pressure groups such as the Society for the Protection of the Unborn Child and Life were formed to lobby against abortion. As we have seen, religious opposition to feminist demands had some success, notably in Ireland. Yet within a comparatively short period of time, where women's groups had a clear campaigning focus and the ability to construct broad networks with sympathetic interest groups to the left and centre of the political spectrum, they became an electoral force to be reckoned with, and one that political parties increasingly felt the need to take account of, as we shall see in the next chapter.

Both Scandinavian-style 'equal rights' or liberal feminism and more radical or socialist feminism played their part in this process. While the former sought to transform patriarchal structures from within, the latter broadened the scope of political campaigning by working through non-hierarchical and loose political networks and introducing new feminist political discourses. The scale and impact of feminist campaigning varied from group to group and from country to country, as we have seen, but its cumulative effect was undoubtedly to transform the west European political landscape. Not only were 'women's issues' such as the availability of abortion and contraception now firmly on the political agenda, but women themselves began to join in party political activity in greater numbers than ever before and to challenge the traditional structures they encountered with growing confidence.

4 Women in political parties

Throughout the twentieth century, political parties have been central to all west European political systems. Within parliamentary democracies, only nationally organised parties have been able to present wide-ranging policy programmes to the electorate and simultaneously put forward candidates in all constituencies or regions across a country. Thus, it has become normal for governments, whether local, regional or national, to be drawn from leading party figures, either from a single party or, in the case of a majority of countries, a number of parties in coalition. As the century developed many electors began to develop firm party attachments, automatically supporting the same party at all elections regardless of who the candidate might be. This has cemented the strong position of parties, and, as a result, the possibility of gaining formal political power working outside of traditional party structures remains slim.

Although parties have become the gatekeepers to the political system, the problem for women (alongside minority groups) has been that many such organisations have proved extremely difficult to break into. Many parties in western Europe were established early in the twentieth century, or even earlier, when only men enjoyed the vote, and as a result party positions (both internal and representative) were initially filled entirely by men. As the franchise became equal (see Table 1, p. 2) women were regarded with hostility as they were perceived as a threat to those holding party positions. Some parties, notably those tied to religion, believed that women should not hold party positions as a point of principle.[1] Even those parties which were formally open to women were often characterised by an aggressive and confrontational style of politics which alienated many women. As a result the proportion of party members who were women remained low, for example in West Germany 85 per cent of party members in 1969 were still male.[2]

WOMEN'S STRATEGIES TO BREAK INTO POLITICAL PARTIES

In broad terms, women developed four main strategies as a response to these barriers. The first approach was to ignore parties altogether as inherently 'masculine' organisations, and to work outside formal political structures, a strategy commonly adopted, as we saw in Chapter 3, during the early years of 'second wave feminism'. In political terms this allowed women to establish their own organisations on their own terms. As Chapter 3 demonstrated, it also led to strong indirect pressure on the formal political system to expand or even to redefine its agenda to incorporate the demands of women. The disadvantage of this strategy was that it did not lead to an increase in the numbers of women on the formal political stage. This was because, as we have noted, many feminists were not inclined to join traditional political parties, yet it was these bodies who provided parliamentary representatives and government ministers. By the late 1970s and early 1980s, there were increasing signs of a change in tactics in a number of countries, as women moved from autonomous groups into mainstream political parties, particularly parties of the left.

Between the separatist strategy of remaining outside political parties altogether and the integrationist approach of joining mainstream party structures, women have adopted two alternative strategies to increase their political influence within political parties. The first such approach has consisted of occasional attempts to establish separate 'women's parties' or form 'women's lists' in elections. This has a superficial attractiveness, as it allows women to work inside the formal political system, but outside the traditional 'masculine' parties. Furthermore, women generally comprise over half of the electorate, forming a potentially large natural constituency for a specifically 'women's' party. However, attempts at forming separate parties or lists, for example in Denmark in 1946 and Norway in the 1970s, have been sporadic and electorally unsuccessful.[3] It is clear that in terms of voting habits, women have behaved similarly to men in developing strong identifications with existing parties, gender proving a relatively unimportant factor in party choice compared with social class and other variables.[4] As a consequence, there has been little or no support to enable specific 'women's' parties to make a breakthrough.

The second alternative approach has been formally to join traditional parties, but to work within their own internal women's organisations. Most parties across western Europe have established special women's groups of various types, either giving women the option to join or automatically enrolling all women party members as members of the women's wing. The advantage of working in such bodies is that women can be encouraged into a formal political party, but within a comfortable atmosphere where men are absent. In addition, many women's organisations have enjoyed direct representation on party governing bodies, enabling the concerns of women to be fed directly to the party leadership. For example, it has been argued in the Netherlands that the women's wings of the political parties have been important in pushing a more radical agenda than the mainstream party bodies on issues regarding women.[5] The strength of the Women's Federation within the Swedish Social Democratic Party is credited with pushing women's issues and the representation of women onto the political agenda a full decade earlier than in most countries. A working committee on women's issues within the party was requested as early as 1960, with equality and equality measures reaching the top of the political agenda by the end of the decade. By 1972 the party leader (and Prime Minister) Olaf Palme claimed at the party congress that the elimination of women's underrepresentation was 'a common task for the entire labour movement',[6] emphasising the direct influence on party policy that women's groups within parties can bring to bear.

Not all authors have viewed party women's organisations in such a positive light. Specifically such groups have been criticised for keeping women away from mainstream party structures, thereby exacerbating the isolation of women, and for concentrating on social activities rather than political. In Britain the Labour Party established women's sections from 1918, with such groups operating at both constituency and more local levels. But it has been argued that these parallel organisational structures for women only served to cut them off from the main party bodies, without giving any direct powers or representation.[7] The main party structures continued to be dominated by men, with women almost totally absent from key party positions at local levels. In Germany, Eva Kolinsky has similarly argued that the separate 'women's track' of politics has had limited political impact on the main party organisation, and has failed to facilitate the entry of women into positions of political power.[8] In both Britain and Germany, party women's organisations have been criticised for becoming little more than glorified social groups, responsible for making the tea, and thereby confirming male prejudices about the 'natural' role of women. Already in the 1920s, Hannah Mitchell, a member of the Independent Labour Party, poured scorn on the first Labour Party women's sections which she labelled as 'a permanent Social Committee, or official cake-maker to the Labour Party'.[9] The existence of such structures, it is argued, have made it more difficult for women to break into positions of power, since 'within the parties, women were expected to hold coffee mornings or help at election times, not bid for the leadership'.[10]

The final approach adopted by women has therefore been to move fully into traditional party political structures. This strategy has become increasingly common since the late 1970s and early 1980s, as large numbers of women politicised by the new wave of feminist movements sought to 'move into the mainstream' and change parties from within. It should be noted that in Scandinavian countries, women were advocating integration into traditional party structures as a viable strategy from a much earlier date. The advantages of this approach could be seen in 1967, when representatives from all parties in Norway joined together in a campaign to improve the number of women elected to municipal councils. The success of this campaign led to an even better-organised repeat four years later. Women members of political parties urged the nomination of more women candidates, and in addition women voters were urged to support women candidates and to cross out the names of men. The result was the 'women's coup' in which women took 15 per cent of all local council seats, including a majority on the councils of Oslo and two other large cities.[11] In more recent times, the large influx of active women joining political parties across a number of countries has increased the pressure to take positive measures to improve the representation of women. As we shall see below, the result has been the implementation of women's quotas across a large number of parties, particularly those on the left.

The advantage then of joining mainstream party political structures is that pressure can be put on party leaders from within to take women's issues and women's representation more seriously. However, such strategies have been criticised since party structures remain male-dominated if not inherently masculine, and, to become successful, women must agree to abide by the existing 'rules of the game'. As a result, any initial thoughts of making parties more women-friendly by changing the party culture from within may be quickly forgotten. It has often been argued that some long-standing women members gradually assume the same characteristics as their male colleagues, and, for example, can be equally hostile to the idea of women standing for political office. In her memoirs, Margaret Thatcher claims that when attempting to be selected as a candidate, not only was she repeatedly interrogated on how she could possibly combine a parliamentary career with family commitments, but that 'it was the women' who were most likely to express such prejudices.[12] More recently, some women joined the campaign against the introduction of women's quotas within the British Labour Party.[13] Thus, it does not necessarily follow that political parties will automatically become more amenable to women just because women become members. It may be that traditional party structures will change women before women change those party structures.

Nevertheless, it is undoubtedly the case that women have made a significant impact in newly formed parties which have not had the time to develop 'traditionally male' internal cultures and practices. Women joining at the start have managed to succeed in defining these parties in more woman-friendly terms. As a result new organisations such as the Green Parties and the Irish Progressive Democrats have attracted large numbers of women into both membership and key positions. As noted in Chapter 3, after the 1987 Bundestag elections, the West German Greens could boast the first parliamentary delegation in German history where women outnumbered men. In 1991, over 40 per cent of Green councillors in Ireland were women, and following the 1992 parliamentary elections, 40 per cent of Progressive Democrat representatives in the Irish Dáil were women, compared with just 7 per cent of the largest party, Fianna Fail.

GROWING MEMBERSHIP, BUT UNDERREPRESENTATION IN LEADING POSITIONS

By the start of the 1990s it was clear that ever-increasing numbers of women were moving into party membership. For example, in Sweden, female membership of the Social Democratic Party had increased from 240,000 in the 1970s to 430,000 by 1985.[14] Five years later women constituted 40 per cent of membership of the Norwegian, British and Dutch Labour Parties. Among parties of the right such figures could be marginally higher; for example, women have been estimated to make up almost 50 per cent of members of the British Conservative Party and over 40 per cent of the French Gaullists. Christian Democratic Parties have been estimated to have the highest proportion of women members of any party in Italy and Norway (though the same has not been true in the Netherlands and Germany).[15]

Despite such high and growing membership figures, the proportion of women on party executives and other key committees has tended to be lower, with men dominating bodies which are often a crucial starting point for a political career. Not only do such committees play an important role in selecting candidates for elected office, but membership of such a committee, and even a leading role, is often seen as a necessary 'apprenticeship' before a party member is considered worthy of selection as a candidate. The pattern that has been repeated throughout western Europe, with the numbers of women on such committees consistently falling well below the overall proportion of members, has therefore been argued to be a central reason for the underrepresentation of women throughout the political system. In Britain, Norris and Lovenduski note that the proportion of women continues to fall off the higher one progresses up the party 'hierarchy', with few women holding important national positions.[16] At the very top, women leaders of political parties have been scarce, particularly the large parties who have a chance of forming or joining a government. A number of authors have even suggested the existence of an 'iron rule': the more powerful a position, the less likely it is to be filled by a woman. This has been argued to apply to all political institutions, including national and local governments (as we shall see in subsequent chapters), but parties are believed by many to hold the key to breaking down such a pattern because of their central role within the political system.

From the late 1970s onwards, a growing number of women party activists responded to the continuing male dominance of key party positions by demanding that women fill a minimum number of places. It was believed that only some form of 'quota' would break down resistance and ensure that women occupied a proportion of prominent party posts which matched the proportion of women members. The pressure for change was sometimes supported by male party members, who believed that the low number of visible party women could have a damaging effect on party image. For example, a report commissioned by the British Labour Party following the 1987 general election defeat concluded that the party was not seen as 'women-friendly', probably because it appeared to be dominated by men.[17] In the French Socialist Party (PS) in the 1970s, a number of activists believed that positive steps had to be taken by the party if it were to attract the support of a greater number of women. A key demand was the introduction of a minimum quota for women for all internal party positions, so that numbers of women in key posts would reflect the overall proportion of women members within the party. The quota was agreed at the 1973 party congress, and although the initial figure of 10 per cent was lower than that demanded by many feminists within the party, it was raised to 15 per cent in 1977 and 20 per cent in 1979.[18] Two years later, the Socialists were propelled back into power, with the presidential and parliamentary elections of 1981 the first occasions in French history when a majority of women had voted for the left.[19]

This outcome suggested a connection between the use of internal measures to boost the number of women in important party positions and greater electoral support from women generally, a crucial conclusion for party leaders and strategists ever alert to ways of expanding their electoral base. By the late 1980s, the principle of internal quotas had been accepted by the German Social Democrats (SPD), Italian Communist Party (PCI) and British Labour Party, all of whom were large opposition parties looking to increase their electoral challenge to dominant right-wing parties. However, by this time, the agenda had again moved forward, with growing demands that women's quotas should apply not only to internal party positions, but also to numbers of parliamentary representatives.

PARLIAMENTARY SELECTION AND THE MOVE TO WOMEN'S QUOTAS

The position of parliamentary candidate is often regarded as the most important party position of all. Only after being selected as a candidate by a large party can most individuals hope to enjoy a career in parliament, and in turn it is usually the case that government ministers are drawn from those who have been elected to parliament. The initial parliamentary selection process is therefore a vital gateway to involvement in national politics, and as a result it has come under close scrutiny in a number of countries over recent years, particularly because the number of women who have been successful in gaining selection has tended to be low.

One interesting argument has been developed by Marila Guadagnini, who has suggested that the chances of women being selected for key decision-making positions such as parliamentary candidates depend in part on the extent of centralisation within a party.[20] Because national party leaderships are more likely to see the advantages of a substantial number of women candidates in terms of party image and possible enhanced electoral support, the number of women ultimately selected may depend on how strong an influence the centre enjoys over local parties in the selection process. Local parties are less likely to see the advantages of a balanced list of candidates, and more likely to look for a series of 'informal qualifications' in a potential candidate, qualifications which women frequently do not hold. Thus, it has been parties with a strong centre or 'core' (such as the Italian Communists and increasingly the Labour Party in Britain) that have been more likely to facilitate the entry of women into parliament in significant numbers rather than parties where parliamentary selection is decentralised to the local level.

Typical informal qualifications looked for by local party selectors include lengthy party service, which does not equate with membership alone but also many years of activism within the party and possibly the holding of local office. A second factor frequently looked for by political parties of all colours is some form of 'personal capital', for example a high profile in the local community; while a third important informal qualification is the ability to speak fluently and confidently in public. It could be argued that all these factors at best discriminate against women and at worst disqualify them from candidature altogether. For example, few women will have had the time to be involved in party activities because of family commitments. The uneven domestic division of family responsibilities has tended to leave the party careers of men unaffected, and it would certainly be unusual for a man to be asked whether having children was incompatible with life in Parliament as Margaret Thatcher was (see above). A high local profile and ability to communicate are attributes which are often associated with a professional occupation, again discriminating against women, who are unlikely to be employed in 'preferred occupations' such as business or the legal profession. For family and employment reasons, therefore, most women are highly unlikely to fulfil the informal selection requirements looked for by party selectors, perhaps explaining why such 'selectorates' in a number of countries continue to claim that there is a shortage of suitable women candidates. As a result, the overwhelming majority of those selected as candidates have been men.

It should also be noted that there are two further factors which have been argued to impede the progress of women into positions as parliamentary candidates in some of the countries under study in this book. The first is the practice of 'multiple mandates', a common feature in France and Ireland, where politicians hold local and national office simultaneously, thereby curtailing the opportunities for others to break into the political system. For example, in Ireland, no fewer than 73 per cent of members of the Dáil elected in 1992 were also members of a local authority.[21] In France this proportion has been similar, with the result being the creation of a self-perpetuating political elite which women find virtually impossible to break into. The second factor which may operate against women concerns the role of trade unions. Such organisations have often been associated with traditional and manufacturing industries, which have a predominantly male work-force. As a result, unions have had overwhelmingly male leaderships, and, where involved in politics, tend to promote male candidates. This has been particularly important in parties such as the British Labour Party where unions have always had an extremely strong influence at national and local levels. For example, in 1983, trade unions 'sponsored' 153 parliamentary candidates, the vast majority of whom (75 per cent) were elected to Parliament, reflecting the strength of unions in Labour's heartland areas. Since only 7 of the 153 union-backed candidates were women,[22] it follows that women were having severe problems gaining selection where union influence (and Labour support) was strong.

In recent years, many parties have come under pressure from women activists and others to counter the informal discrimination involved in parliamentary selection procedures. The key demand has been that parties should take a central decision to implement a national women's quota, ensuring that a certain proportion of their parliamentary candidates are women. The leading country in the move to establish quotas for parliamentary representatives has been Norway, and there can be little doubt as to the success of the process. Quotas were first introduced by the Socialist Left Party in 1975, which introduced a rule whereby 40 per cent of their parliamentary candidates must be women. At the following three elections (1977, 1981 and 1985), 50 per cent women's representation was achieved, albeit in the context of a small parliamentary delegation. More significantly, the same quota rule was adopted by the Labour Party after 1981, who met the minimum quota in 1985 (see Table 3), and achieved 50 per cent women's representation in 1989, a period in which they were the largest party in Norway. Finally, the liberal Centre Party followed suit in 1989, and also saw a significant rise in the numbers of women within their parliamentary party. In overall terms, the period saw fourfold growth in the number of women in the Norwegian Storting (parliament), from 9 per cent in 1969 to 39 per cent by 1993. By contrast, the same period in Britain, where no party introduced quotas, saw the number of women in Parliament increase from 4 per cent in 1970 to little over 9 per cent by 1992.

Partly as a result of the success of quotas in Norway, major parties in other countries soon followed suit. In Denmark, the Social Democrats introduced a gender quota in 1988, with the proportion of female representatives increasing from 24 per cent in 1987 to 39 per cent in 1994. The Dutch Labour Party set a 25 per cent quota in 1987, which was increased to 33 per cent in 1992, while the Spanish Socialists (PSOE) saw a big increase in the number of women elected to the national parliament after introducing a 25 per cent quota in 1988. In

Table 3 The impact of women's quotas in Norway

Party	% Women in parliament before quotas introduced	Quota introduced	% Women in parliament after quotas introduced
Social Left	–	1975	50 (1977)
Labour Party	26 (1977)	1981–3	42 (1985)
Centre Party	17 (1985)	1989	44 (1993)
% Women in Parliament	9 (1969)		39 (1993)

Source: L. Karvonen and P. Selle, *Women in Nordic Politics: Closing the Gap* (Aldershot: Dartmouth, 1995), p. 35.

Britain, the decision of the Labour Party to introduce 'all-women shortlists' for half of all winnable seats before the 1997 general election ensured a significant increase in the representation of women not only in the parliamentary Labour Party (up from 14 per cent to 24 per cent), but also within Parliament as a whole (up from 9 per cent to 18 per cent). Meanwhile the decision of the French Socialists to reserve 30 per cent of constituencies for women prior to the 1997 election was the main reason behind an increase in the overall proportion of women in the French parliament from just 6 per cent to over 10 per cent. In neither of these two countries was there any previous history of such affirmative action, but the undoubted success of the strategy in 1997 led to similar positive action for regional elections in France in 1998 and regional elections in Scotland and Wales in 1999.

A LEFT–RIGHT DIVIDE?

Despite the overwhelmingly successful outcome of women's quotas in boosting women's representation across western Europe, it is clear from the above examples that is has been parties of the left who have tended to implement such a strategy. Right-wing parties (including those in Norway) and a number of liberal parties have objected to positive discrimination for women, believing that there should always be a free choice of candidates and that they should be selected on the basis of merit, without the 'artificial' constraint of quotas. In Britain, a leading Conservative politician, David Hunt, warned in 1995 that Labour's policy of positive discrimination in favour of women was 'window-dressing', 'gesture politics' and 'could have diametrically the opposite effect [to that intended]'. Some women have also argued that the political status of women will become diminished if they are seen to rely on quotas to be selected, for example a prominent woman in the British Liberal Democrats, Diana Maddock argued that women should have 'equal treatment not special treatment'.[23]

However, the implementation of quotas has contributed to a clear pattern in virtually all of our ten countries: women are consistently more likely to enter parliament from parties of the left than parties of the right. While many left-wing parties have taken positive action to boost women's representation, the right continues to rely on exhorting local party organisations to select more women candidates, efforts that often have little effect, as one might expect given the informal barriers to women's selection discussed above. For example, in the British General Election of 1997, Labour's all women shortlists resulted in an increase in the number of women MPs from 37 to over 100 (24 per cent of the total), while the number of Conservative women MPs fell from 20 to just 13 (8 per cent of the total), a smaller number than elected in 1970. In the French election of 1997, the Socialists saw their proportion of women MPs rise to 15 per cent, compared with just 5 per cent for the right-wing Gaullist RPR. And similar discrepancies between parties of left and right have been apparent in Italy, Spain and Germany. We should also note that women's representation is highest of all in the Green Parties, with the introduction of 50 per cent women's quotas reflected in women outnumbering men in parliamentary delegations in Germany, the Netherlands and Sweden.

In the Netherlands and Scandinavia, parties of the right tend to have fewer women MPs than parties of the left, but the discrepancy is not as striking as elsewhere. This may reflect the increased pressure on parties of the right to select more women, if only as a response to their political opponents. For example, women comprise 30 per cent of Conservative MPs in Norway, 34 per cent of Christian Democrat MPs in the Netherlands and 43 per cent of Christian Democrat MPs in Sweden, despite the absence of formal quotas. Although these levels remain lower than those of the respective Labour or Social Democrat Parties in each case, the figures are strikingly higher than the single-figure percentages achieved by parties of the right in Britain, France and Italy. A contributing factor may be the use of systems of proportional representation and party lists, which make it easier for party selectors to include a significant number of women (this factor will be considered in greater depth in Chapter 8). It may also be the case that the notion of a woman MP has now become accepted as 'normal' in Scandinavia, which reduces the need for specific quotas. Finally, the success of female politicians such as Gro Harlem Bruntland in Norway may also have encouraged more women to put themselves forward as candidates, though such a pattern appears not to have occurred in Britain despite Margaret Thatcher's 11 years as Prime Minister.

CONCLUSION

Women have made substantial progress within political parties, particularly since the 1970s. It is noteworthy that much of this progress took place in the years immediately following the rise of 'second wave feminism', suggesting that many women used such movements as a springboard into the formal political process, and also that parties became more willing to accept women as members and activists. Campaigning for quotas has provided a focus for a large number of women within parties in the 1980s and 1990s, and has undoubtedly been successful in increasing the number of women elected to both internal party positions and parliament. However, the success of women's quotas may have clouded the issue of whether parties have in reality become 'women-friendly', and there undoubtedly remain both women and men in all parties who remain firmly opposed to the use of quotas as a means of increasing women's political representation. In general, it would be true to say that outside recently formed parties there is little evidence of major change away from traditional structures, particularly at a local level. There is also a striking absence of women at the very highest political levels, a subject to which we now turn.

5 Women in government

A major study of key political leaders in western Europe in the post-war period thought fit to include just three women out of a total of 71 major figures.[1] Included in the volume were two out of the three women who have succeeded in becoming prime ministers in western Europe: Margaret Thatcher, British Prime Minister from 1979 to 1990, and Gro Harlem Bruntland, Norwegian Prime Minister on three occasions in the 1980s and 1990s. A third Prime Minister, Edith Cresson, who briefly headed the French government from 1991–2, was not included. How can we explain the absence of women in leading positions? The first part of the explanation must relate to issues covered in previous chapters, particularly the difficulty women have had in gaining selection by political parties as parliamentary candidates. Unless they have first been elected to parliament, it is highly unlikely that women will enter government, since the few who do become ministers without a parliamentary background tend to require a high profile in business or the trade unions, both of which are heavily male-dominated. But the low number of women in parliament (see Table 8, p. 105 for numbers of women MPs in the ten countries between 1945 and 1999) forms only a part of the explanation for the lack of women in the very top political jobs. As the data below reveals, women are beginning to enter national governments in growing numbers, but the posts they occupy remain disproportionately at the lower end of the ministerial 'hierarchy'. At the beginning of this new millennium, there is still an almost total absence of women in the very top posts in government.

WOMEN IN CABINET POSITIONS BY COUNTRY

It is a feature of national governments that a small group of ministers, often known as the 'cabinet', fill key government positions and take

Table 4 Women in the cabinet by country, December 1997

Country	Ministers in the cabinet	Women in the cabinet	% Women
Sweden	22	11	50.0
Norway	19	9	47.4
France	17	6	35.3
Netherlands	14	4	28.6
Spain	15	4	26.7
Denmark	20	5	25.0
UK	22	5	22.7
Ireland	15	3	20.0
Italy	22	3	13.6
Germany	18	2	11.1
Total	*184*	*52*	*28.3*

Source: R. Katz and R. Koole (eds), *Political Data Yearbook 1998* (*European Journal of Political Research*, vol. 34, nos 3–4).

major policy decisions. Of course within a cabinet all ministers are not necessarily equal, and an examination of the posts which are held by women reveals a number of interesting features (see p. 58). First we look at the total number of women cabinet ministers by country (Table 4), and it is once again clear that Scandinavia leads the way in terms of women's involvement in the political system.

In late 1997 Sweden was at the top of the list, with a cabinet that had featured a 50:50 gender balance since 1994. In second place was neighbouring Norway, not far behind with a near gender balance in its cabinet. Indeed it was Norway which saw the first 'women's government', when Gro Harlem Brundtland appointed eight women to her cabinet in 1986. It should also be noted that the comparatively low proportion of women in the cabinet in Denmark (25 per cent) marked a temporary blip between proportions of 35 per cent reached in 1994 and again after 1998. Thus, it is the Scandinavian countries which continue to lead the way in terms of women in leading government positions, although at the end of the 1990s, a number of other countries started rapidly to narrow the gap.

It was the elections of 1997 and 1998 that resulted in significant increases in the proportion of women in the governments in three of western Europe's major countries, namely, France, Britain and Germany. In all three cases a new party or coalition took over, and the new government was formed from parties of the left. The pattern of change began in Britain, where there had been no women ministers at all in the first cabinet after the fall of Margaret Thatcher from power in 1990. By early 1997 two women had reached the cabinet (out of 23), but this low total was to more than double to five under the new Labour government of Tony Blair. In France, the change was even more dramatic, with new Prime Minister Lionel Jospin increasing the proportion of women in the cabinet from just 7 per cent to more than 30 per cent. As a result, France enjoyed the third-highest proportion of women in its cabinet by late 1997, whereas it had been bottom of the table in 1996. In Germany, which dropped to the bottom of the table by late 1997, the new 'Red-Green' government elected in 1998 included more than 30 per cent of women at all levels, again a dramatic change from the low number of women in the government of Chancellor Kohl's Christian Democrats.

As outlined above, in all three countries it was the left who were returning to power following a lengthy absence, and it is noteworthy that the idea of 'change' played an important part in each election campaign. In Britain, Labour became 'New' Labour and campaigned against the 'sleaze' of the ruling Conservative Party, while in France the Socialists had a new image, a new programme and a pledge to renew democratic life, which included equality for men and women in politics.[2] In both France and Britain, photographs of the new prime ministers surrounded by large numbers of successful women candidates featured prominently in post-election coverage, and it was clear that the issue of women's involvement in politics had to an extent been incorporated into the new, successful, political message of the left.

In many ways this development in France, Britain and Germany only mirrored what had already occurred in the Scandinavian countries a decade or so earlier. Given that Sweden, Norway and Denmark have tended to be dominated by Social Democrat Parties, there would seem to be clear grounds for arguing that the number of women in government is largely dependent on the political complexion of that government. However, it should be pointed out that there are exceptions to a straightforward left–right pattern. In Norway, the Conservative coalition maintained high levels of women in the cabinet after Bruntland fell from power in 1989. In Spain, the proportion of women in the government increased in 1996 when the right-wing Popular Party took over from the Socialists (though the increase in numbers was admittedly more marginal than that in France or Britain the following year when the left replaced the right). The proportion of women in the Spanish cabinet in late 1996 was double that in Italy, where the same year had seen the return of the left to government after an absence of almost 50 years. Here, the political representation of women did not appear to feature in the renewed political programme of the left, though the number of women in the cabinet did significantly increase after a second left-wing government was formed in October 1998. This change in Italy left all ten countries in our study with at least 20 per cent of women in their respective cabinets by early 1999, and Ireland and the United Kingdom at the bottom of the table.

WOMEN IN CABINET POSITIONS BY POST

It has often been suggested that the higher one moves up the political hierarchy, the number of women that can be found becomes smaller and smaller. Thus, women may be moving into national governments, but the most powerful positions remain overwhelmingly dominated by men. This idea, termed either 'hierarchical marginalisation' or 'the law of increasing disproportion', has been put forward over many decades. For example in the 1950s, Duverger had already noted that not only was the political role of women 'extremely small' but that it 'grows still smaller as we approach the centre of political leadership'.[3] Similar comments have been made in every decade during the post-war period, right up to the end of the 1990s, and such a pattern is immediately apparent from Table 5, which again brings together data at the end of 1997 from the ten countries under study in this book.

It is immediately clear from Table 5 that at the end of the twentieth century women were still almost entirely absent from leading positions within government. Most obviously, there were no female prime ministers at the end of 1997, and indeed there had only ever been three in the history of the ten countries within the remit of this study: Margaret Thatcher in the United Kingdom (1979–90), Edith Cresson in France (1991–92) and Gro Harlem Bruntland in Norway (1981, 1986–89, 1990–96). The leadership style of the three women prime ministers will be examined below. To that short list one could add Mary Robinson, elected President of the Irish Republic in 1990 (and indeed her successor Mary McAleese), but the post of Irish President has remained largely ceremonial, in many ways not unlike the modern day role of a monarch. Having said that, the surprise election of a woman to such a prominent position did clearly mark something of a watershed in Ireland, and when Robinson moved on to become UN Commissioner for Human Rights in 1997, not only were four of the five candidates for president women, but the 'token man' finished bottom of the poll with less than five per cent of the vote!

If it is usually the prime minister who is in overall control of government policy, those who become foreign ministers and leading

Table 5 Women in cabinet positions in the ten countries by post, December 1997

Post	Ministers in the cabinet	Number of women	% Women
Prime ministers	10	0	0
Deputy prime ministers	6	1	17
Leading foreign ministers	10	1	10
Leading finance ministers	10	1	10
Other finance or trade ministers	18	2	11
Defence ministers	10	0	0
Home affairs ministers	9	0	0
Agriculture ministers	11	2	18
Housing, transport, dev't, employment and labour	26	9	35
Health, welfare, education and social affairs	31	16	52
Justice/culture/environment ministers	26	16	62
Other ministers*	17	4	23
Total ministers in cabinet	**184**	**52**	**28**

Source: R. Katz and R. Koole (eds), *Political Data Yearbook 1998* (*European Journal of Political Research*, vol. 34, nos 3–4)

Note: * Mainly regional ministers and ministers responsible for relations with parliament.

economics or finance ministers will also have a degree of influence over policy that is substantially greater than that enjoyed by most of their colleagues. Again, we must note that virtually all of these important posts were held by men at the end of 1997. The only women in these prestigious positions were the Swedish Minister of Foreign Affairs and the Danish Minister for Economic Affairs, again marking out the Scandinavian countries from the others in this study. In the five largest and most influential countries in western Europe (Britain, France, Germany, Italy and Spain), there were no women at all in the three posts at the summit of the political system.

It is not only the top political posts from which women are almost completely absent. In late 1997 there were certain portfolios which remained dominated by men, and a number of ministries in various countries where no woman had ever been 'in charge'. For example, there were no female Defence ministers and no female Home Affairs ministers as we approached the end of the century, suggesting that such posts, often encompassing responsibility for the armed forces and police forces, were still universally regarded as a male domain.

There were only two lower-ranking finance or trade ministers, of whom one, Margaret Beckett, was removed from her post and replaced by a man in the first cabinet change in the UK after the election of the 'new' Labour government in 1997. Perhaps what links the posts where women remain noticeable by their absence is not simply that they are regarded as influential in policy terms, but that they often act as a 'stepping stone' to the very top government posts. For example, ministers who have had responsibility for economics, finance or trade are in a much better position to move up the political ladder than a minister who has served in a health or education ministry. Thus, not only are women missing from the very top levels of government, but they are also absent from the 'second tier' of posts, suggesting that the number of women leaders is unlikely to increase significantly in the near future.

Traditionally it has been the case that women who have reached government have been placed in 'soft' ministries such as social affairs, welfare, education and health. Several authors have termed these positions 'ministries of reproduction', suggesting that placing women in such roles as minister for health merely replicates the compartmentalised position of women throughout society. In the early postwar years, a very large percentage of the small number of women cabinet ministers found themselves in such posts, and by the 1990s it was the case that over 50 per cent of these ministerial positions were filled by women. One explanation for such a large percentage is that these ministries may simply be regarded by men as less important and powerful than others. Nevertheless, with the post-war growth of welfare states in western Europe and Scandinavia, ministries such as health have expanded and now often enjoy extremely large budgets. Furthermore it is undoubtedly the case that many women see these areas as more important than traditionally powerful ministries such as defence or foreign affairs.

It is clear from the data in Table 5 that women have now broken into a number of positions beyond the traditional 'soft' sphere, and that this further tranche includes some traditionally male areas. Thus, at the end of 1997, women not only comprised a majority of ministers for justice and environment, but also a significant minority of labour and employment ministers. To an extent this emerging pattern breaks down the traditional argument that women in government will be confined to traditional roles, since if education, health and social affairs can be described as ministries of 'reproduction', employment, housing and labour could be summarised as ministries of 'production'. It is also the case that employment in particular is now regarded as a key issue in western Europe, and that to have such a high-profile ministry headed by a woman (as in France) must be a sign that women are no longer being confined to roles regarded by men as unimportant. However, it remains the case that in general these ministries are less powerful than, for example, financial portfolios. We should also note the 'shrinking institutions' thesis, which suggests that while women are now moving into certain ministerial positions previously regarded as male domains, these posts are simultaneously becoming less powerful because of the growing influence of multinational companies and financial institutions over areas such as employment.

WOMEN AS PRIME MINISTERS

As mentioned above, only three women have risen to the position of prime minister in our ten countries over the entire post-war period. From this small number, is it possible to draw any conclusions as to why certain women rise to the top, or about the way in which women leaders behave? The longest-serving female leader was Margaret Thatcher, who became the first woman head of government in modern Europe when she became Prime Minister of the UK in 1979, lasting for 11 years between 1979 and 1990. Thatcher had served in the Conservative cabinet from 1970 to 1974 as Minister for Education, but it was a major surprise when she was elected leader of the party in 1975, defeating the sitting party leader and former prime minister, Edward Heath. A large part of Thatcher's appeal was based on her ideological position to the right of the party, and she capitalised on the failure of any other major figure to challenge Heath's leadership, an unusual example of a woman putting herself forward when a number of men held back.

After the Conservatives returned to power in 1979, Thatcher soon became known for her strong leadership style, not only taking on the traditional power of trade unions such as the National Union of Mineworkers, but also never hesitating before removing government ministers who did not share her views. By the summer of 1983, almost half of the cabinet team of 1979 had been replaced, the majority of them Conservative 'wets' who believed in old-style consensus rather than Thatcher's 'conviction' politics. Towards the end of her time as prime minister, Thatcher's increasingly autocratic governing style led to the resignations of key ministers such as Nigel Lawson and Geoffrey Howe, who had served as Chancellor and Foreign Secretary respectively. Ultimately this tendency to ride roughshod over even senior ministers was to prove fatal for Thatcher's career as prime minister; in 1990 she was essentially removed by her own party in mid-term after being challenged for the Conservative Party leadership by Michael Heseltine, who himself had resigned from the government in 1985. But despite her inglorious fall from power, we should remember that Thatcher won an unprecedented three successive general elections as Conservative leader, and her strong leadership style was widely admired by many inside and outside her party.

It should be noted that Thatcher completely failed to promote any women to her cabinet in her time as prime minister. Her first cabinet in 1979 and her last in 1990 contained no women apart from herself, and only one other woman reached the cabinet in the intervening years. Such was Thatcher's legacy that her successor as Conservative Party leader and prime minister, John Major, did not include any women in his first cabinet in late 1990. Thatcher's failure to promote women is in stark contrast to the records of both Norwegian Prime Minister Gro Harlem Bruntland and former French Prime Minister, Edith Cresson. On becoming prime minister for the second time in 1986, Bruntland included a world-record eight women in her 18-strong cabinet, while Cresson included no fewer than six women in her cabinet after becoming prime minister in 1991. This does suggest that Thatcher may have been unusual in her reluctance to promote other women, though with such a small number of women leaders we cannot yet draw any clear conclusions.

Gro Harlem Bruntland had sat in Parliament for just four years when she became Prime Minister of Norway for the first time in 1981, but her parents had both been politically influential in the past, with her father serving as Minister for Social Affairs and later for Defence for many years. Such family networks have been a prominent feature of some less developed countries (for example, the Gandhis in India and the Bhuttos in Pakistan have provided male and female leaders since the war) but they have not been common in post-war western Europe. Bruntland had also previously served as a government minister, and became deputy leader of the Labour Party in 1975, but was still the youngest ever head of a government in Norway when she assumed the party leadership in 1981. Bruntland initially lasted only a few months as prime minister, but returned to the post five years later, and by 1996 she had served approximately ten years in the top post. Like Thatcher, Bruntland's leadership style was criticised as arrogant, direct and aggressive,[4] but unlike Thatcher she promoted both other women and women's interests. Her work on the environment and nuclear disarmament also hints at a distinct female agenda in policy terms, which was totally absent throughout Thatcher's time as UK Prime Minister.

The third woman prime minister, Edith Cresson, lasted only ten months in the job after being selected by President Mitterrand for the post in late 1991. Like Bruntland, Cresson appointed a record number of women to her cabinet, despite the extremely low numbers of women at the time in the French National Assembly and Senate. However, Cresson soon became deeply unpopular among both politicians and the public for her leadership style, particularly her comments on Japanese businessmen and her observation that a quarter of English, German and American men were 'gay'. Some observers have questioned whether the vehemence of this criticism reflected the fact that Cresson was a woman, and point to the widely circulated (but unproved) rumours from the outset suggesting she owed her position to a more than close friendship with François Mitterrand. What cannot be denied is that when Cresson resigned as prime minister in 1992, she had achieved popularity ratings that set a new record low for any French leader. However, it is interesting that, like Thatcher and Bruntland, it was Cresson's combative leadership style which drew most criticism. This tends to suggest either that successful women politicians need to be extremely tough to reach the top, or that a still largely male political world disapproves of women who display strong leadership, even though the very same quality is to be admired in a male leader.

WOMEN'S MINISTRIES

An interesting development in a number of governments in the 1980s and 1990s has been the creation of some sort of 'women's ministry', to give a higher profile to women's issues. Such ministries have also provided an opportunity for many women to be given government posts, though there has been a huge variation in the exact form and influence of such bodies in different countries. Perhaps the best-known Ministry of Women's Rights was established in France under Yvette Roudy after the Socialists returned to power in 1981. This became a highly visible ministry which set out to enhance the position of women in employment, improve access to contraception and abortion, provide information on women's issues and generally increase the power and autonomy of women throughout France while opposing sexism.[5] Laws were soon passed strengthening the rights of women in the workplace, while a nationwide campaign was launched to encourage family planning. This included the distribution of a million brochures on contraceptive usage, information which was previously unavailable. After a year of this campaign, family planning consultations doubled and 88 new family planning centres had been created. In addition, 140 'National Centres for Information on the Rights of Women' were also established throughout France,[6] which further enhanced the visibility of the ministry.

In Spain, an 'Institute for Women' was established in 1983 as part of the Ministry of Culture (later Ministry of Social Affairs). By the early 1990s its budget had grown significantly to exceed £10 million.[7] The functions of the institute have included co-ordination of equality policies, running employment, training and health programmes, publishing information and giving grants to women's organisations across Spain. Similar bodies were also established within the country's autonomous regions. In West Germany, a new Department for Women's Affairs was created in 1986 when 'women' were added to the responsibilities of the Ministry for Youth, Family and Health (in 1991 a separate ministry was created for women and youth). Again, the department was given an extensive remit, including checking new legislation for its effect on women and initiating legislation to improve the position of women in areas such as employment.

Women's ministries elsewhere have been formed in a more half-hearted way or not established at all despite earlier promises. A Ministry for Women's Affairs was established in Ireland in 1982, but suffered from a lack of resources and did not have cabinet status. Although there were some reforms in terms of equal rights legislation, other promises on equal access for women to a range of facilities were unfulfilled and the ministry was abolished in 1987.[8] In the United Kingdom, Labour had promised a 'Ministry for Women' in their 1987 manifesto, based on the French and (West) German models. There was to be a cabinet minister specifically responsible for women, who would monitor all government legislation for its impact on women, while initiating legislation to benefit women. By the time of Labour's election victory in 1997, this promise had been severely watered down, and though there is now technically a 'Minister for Women', there is no separate ministry and the minister herself is simultaneously responsible for another major area of government policy.[9] Nevertheless, this in itself is an advance on the previous government; Angela Rumbold denied that she was Minister for Women and concentrated on her portfolio as Minister of State at the Home Office.

In the Netherlands, rather than establish a separate women's department or ministry, successive governments have attempted to integrate issues such as equal rights and equal opportunities for women into the mainstream government agenda. In many ways this approach has followed the 'state feminism' of Scandinavian countries such as Norway, where an 'Equal Status Council' was established as early as 1972 to advocate equality in business, education, community and family life.[10] A raft of legislation followed, notably the 1978 Equal Status Act which regulates areas such as employment, education, advertising and family life, outlawing any form of discrimination. In the Netherlands a succession of committees and policy programmes on 'emancipation' were established from the 1970s onwards, which have taken as a starting point the structural imbalance of power relations between women and men. Policies have not only included subsidising a variety of women's groups, but also exerting pressure on parties to nominate more women, including offering financial inducements. According to Leijenaar, the government has played a 'crucial role' in creating a positive attitude to the political integration of women.[11]

The success of government initiatives in Scandinavian countries and the Netherlands prompted a more general shift towards the 'mainstreaming' of gender issues by the end of the twentieth century. For example, the British government announced in May 1998 that all policy documents and legislative changes would contain an assessment on their impact on women, and that civil servants should consult women's groups when formulating policy. Such initiatives aim to counter the traditional male bias in policy making, and have been launched across western Europe in the late 1990s, largely inspired by the increasingly influential European Union. We will examine the concept of 'mainstreaming' and the equality programmes of the EU in more detail in Chapter 7.

CONCLUSION

By the end of the twentieth century, there had only been a tiny number of women leaders in western Europe, a pattern which is echoed by the complete absence of women from the presidency (and vice-presidency) of the United States. The small number of women leaders makes it difficult if not impossible to generalise about the behaviour of women in leadership positions, and how it might differ from that of their male counterparts. In addition, the more important government portfolios such as foreign affairs, defence, home and economic affairs, which are seen as stepping stones to the very top post, remain totally male-dominated, suggesting that few women will rise to the position of prime minister in the immediate future. What is clear is that women have moved beyond the 'soft' ministries of education, health and welfare, to which they had traditionally been restricted. In addition, women's policies in general are now seen as more important by governments, though this development may reflect the battle for women's votes rather than the influence of women ministers.

6   Women in local government

Have women in the past three or four decades found it as difficult to exercise political power at a local level as they have at a national level? There might be an assumption that women would find it easier to combine their family responsibilities and work patterns with local political activity. Furthermore, it has been argued that the areas of policy covered by local government, embracing education, social and welfare services and health, are of particular interest to women. However, as we shall see, in the great majority of our countries women play no greater role in local than in national politics. Furthermore, as at the national level, a pattern of 'hierarchichal marginalisation' applies – the more important the position, the fewer the number of women who are to be found in occupation. This can be seen most strikingly at local and regional level by looking at elected or even appointed mayors and at council and regional assembly leaders. The percentages of women holding such positions are disproportionately low right across western Europe. Though it is not always easy to collect extensive data from all ten countries on the gender make-up of local and regional councils and on whether women cluster on particular committees or take on particular portfolios, the available evidence strongly suggests that women exercise much greater responsibility in the fields of education, social services and the arts than in finance, transport or economic planning.

EXTENT OF REPRESENTATION ON LOCAL COUNCILS

Figures drawn from 1996–99 show that in only three of our countries – Britain, France and Italy – was the percentage of women elected as local councillors significantly greater than the percentage of women serving as national deputies or MPs. In Britain, after the 1997 general election, the percentage of women MPs almost doubled from 10 per cent to 18 per cent. Meanwhile, the proportion of women councillors in England and Wales rose from around 24 per cent in the mid-1990s to over 26 per cent in 1999, though in Scotland it was 22 per cent and in Northern Ireland only 17 per cent. In France, which boasts more local councillors than any other European country – over half a million – there were nearly 11 per cent of women deputies in the National Assembly in 1997 but double that percentage, nearly 23 per cent, at local council level. And in Italy, where the percentage of women at national level remained at only 11 per cent in the late 1990s, there were over 19 per cent of women councillors at local level by the middle of the decade, though this figure dropped to 15.2 per cent in 1999.

Conversely, in the Netherlands over a third of the Lower Chamber at national level are women, compared with just under 23 per cent of women on local councils, and in Germany the percentage of women in the Bundestag is 31 per cent, whereas only 25 per cent of local councillors are women. That pattern is repeated in Denmark, where 37 per cent of the National Assembly are women, as against only 27 per cent at local level and, to a lesser extent, in Spain where women comprise almost a quarter of the national Cortes, but only 21.5 per cent of local councillors. Data from the early 1990s in Norway suggests a similar pattern to Denmark, with 36 per cent of women elected to the Storting (the National Assembly) but just under 30 per cent to local councils. In Ireland the percentages at national (12 per cent) and at local level (16 per cent) are among the lowest of our ten countries, with not much difference between them, and Sweden's figures for national and local levels of representation are also similar, but there the percentages of women at national (43 per cent) and at local level (41 per cent) are the highest in the world.[1]

It is perhaps surprising to find that in the majority of our countries women find it harder to gain election at local than at national level. One explanation is that in countries with proportional representation electoral systems, a reasonable number of women are placed on national party lists to provide balance and to appeal to a wide range of interests. Parties in some countries, such as the Danish People's Socialist Party, have adopted quotas for women at national level; others, as in Sweden, and the Green Party in Germany, have opted for 'zipper' systems (one male candidate, one female in order down the list) to boost the numbers of women candidates. In Norway, all political parties aim to include 50 per cent of women in their national lists. But while it is possible for parties and for governments to take action to encourage greater numbers of women at national level, local political decision making can be a much more decentralised process, with local interest groups, often composed largely of males, playing a much more dominant role. This point is supported by data from recent English local elections which suggests that women are less likely than men to be selected by the major parties to contest their most winnable seats, and that one reason for this is that party selection committees are likely to be dominated by men.[2]

In both France and Britain the system of voting at national level is by majority; absolute majority in France and simple majority (or 'plurality' – see Chapter 8) in Britain. The consequence is that levels of female representation at national level are much lower than in countries with proportional representation systems but they are roughly similar at local level. There are several factors helping women to gain election in local as opposed to national elections in Britain and France. Women often find it easier in Britain to be adopted as candidates for multi-member wards on district councils rather than for single-member wards, and may feel more confident about contesting such wards. Furthermore, local campaigns are both less costly to fight and easier to fit into a domestic or part-time work schedule than national election campaigns. In larger electoral districts and major cities in France, a proportional voting system is used, which makes it easier for women to be elected. In both France and Italy in the past 20 years, there have been attempts to increase the numbers of women elected at local level by setting minimum quotas for female candidates in local elections. However, the courts in both countries subsequently ruled that such practices were unconstitutional. In 1982, France passed a law establishing a quota of 25 per cent female candidates on party lists for municipal elections. After a legal challenge, the Constitutional Council in September of the same year ruled that such legislation was incompatible with the principle of equality and was therefore unconstitutional. In 1993 in Italy, two electoral laws were implemented, the first stating that on party lists neither sex could be represented by more than 75 per cent of all candidates, and the second laying down that male and female candidates should appear alternately on party lists. However, two years later the Constitutional Court declared the laws unconstitutional because they had violated equal treatment legislation.[3]

Research carried out in France has suggested that women are more likely than men to serve only one or two terms of office, and therefore they are less likely to be successful in building up a strong local following. A study of town councillors in Piedmont, Italy, found that it was more difficult for women to get into office than men and that the main obstacles they faced were the reconciliation of family duties with work and political activity, lack of encouragement from political parties and from other women, insufficient financial resources and restricted networks of connections. These findings are also supported by data from English local elections.[4] In Ireland, there is an added difficulty for women in that it is quite normal for national politicians to combine this role with being a local councillor. In 1992 nearly three-quarters of Dáil representatives also served as local councillors, making it as hard for women to gain selection for winnable local seats as for safe national ones. However, they were much more likely to be adopted as local candidates and to be elected in an urban conurbation such as Dublin than in a rural area, and this is also true in countries as diverse as Spain and Sweden. In Dublin in 1991, 21 per cent of councillors elected were female, roughly twice the average percentage of female councillors at that time, and the Madrid regional council in Spain, in 1995, had the highest percentage of women members in the country at nearly 30 per cent. In 1998, Stockholm city council had virtually equal male and female representation. Similarly in Britain, women were more likely to win seats in London and on the large urban councils than on small and rural bodies.

This positive correlation between female representation and the degree of urbanisation of a region or locality was noted recently in a report by Patrizia Dini, an Italian delegate to the Chamber of Regions of the Congress of Local and Regional Authorities of Europe in 1999. She argued that it was true both in France and in Germany; for example, in Baden Wurttemberg, in Germany, the larger the municipality, the higher the percentage of female representation, confirming, as she asserts 'the positive correlation between urban lifestyle and women's participation in political life'. Clearly, we need more research to pinpoint exactly what factors make it easier for women to access political power in larger cities. Are women in urban areas more likely to be better educated, employed in professional occupations which allow them time off for council meetings, and more interested in politics than their rural sisters? Or are the political parties themselves easier to break into in urban rather than in rural areas and more sympathetic to women as local representatives? In Italy, Patrizia Dini notes a low rate of female participation in the more rural south of the country, as against large numbers of women representatives in more urbanised regions which are politically 'red' such as in Emilia Romagna, Tuscany and Umbria.[5]

Can we assume from this example that parties of the left are more likely to adopt women in winnable local and regional seats than those of the centre or right or religious parties? The report produced in 1994 by the European Network, 'Women in Decision-making' did not produce clear evidence, in its survey of EU members, to bear this out. Instead it revealed that in Denmark and in Germany, it was the Green Party which had the highest percentage of female representatives both at regional and at local level in the early 1990s. Figures for percentages of women councillors representing socialist parties and centre-right parties were not that dissimilar.[6] This supports the finding made by Rallings and Thrasher in their study of local elections in Britain that the party with the best record in recruiting women candidates in recent times has been the Greens. At the 1989 county elections no fewer than 35 per cent of the party's candidates were women, and in the 1990 shire and metropolitan district elections, four out of ten Green party candidates were female. However, in the following year's local elections, while a third of Liberal Democrat candidates were women, the percentage for both the Labour and Conservative Parties was less impressive, at 27 per cent.[7]

The highest percentages of female representation below national level are to be found on regional councils, in those countries which have a regional tier of government. In Sweden, nearly 48 per cent of regional councillors are female, and the figure is nearly 39 per cent in Norway and 31 per cent in Denmark. 30 per cent of the Dutch provincial councillors are female, and nearly 30 per cent of the German Länder parliaments. Only Spain (just under 20 per cent) and Italy (16 per cent) have regional percentages of women representatives lower than the proportion at local council level. Until recently, there was no regional tier of government in the United Kingdom. However, it is interesting to note that elections to the Scottish and Welsh Assemblies, held in 1999, resulted in considerably higher percentages of women members, 40 per cent in Wales and 38 per cent in Scotland, than previous local elections in those areas. One of the major reasons for this was the selection procedure adopted by the Labour Party, whereby two constituencies were 'twinned' to ensure the selection of a male and a female candidate. This process was facilitated by the fact that the assemblies were new entities, and thus there were no incumbents. At present, there are no plans within the Labour Party to adopt this process for other elections, local or national.

Of course, percentages are not the whole story. They give us an overall picture, but because there are more places on regional and local councils than in national assemblies, far greater numbers of women are serving as councillors and are gaining experience at local and regional level than at national level, and female levels of representation on local bodies have been steadily rising since the 1980s. In addition, governments have taken measures to appoint greater numbers of women to advisory and official bodies at local and national level. In Denmark, parliament passed a law in 1985 stating that all public committees must have a gender-balanced composition: any organisations represented on a committee had to nominate both a man and a woman for each position and it would be up to the minister responsible to select candidates to achieve an overall gender balance. This led to a great increase in female representation on public committees from 12 per cent to 37 per cent. In Norway, the target for female representation on public bodies is 40 per cent, and data banks of the names of suitably qualified women are held to ensure that the target is met. In Ireland, in the 1990s the Department of Equality and Law Reform has laid down a 40 per cent guideline for the appointment of women to public bodies, though there is no mechanism to enforce the target. In Britain, by the late 1990s, women held 28 per cent of publicly appointed posts, and the new Labour government set itself the target of increasing that to 40 per cent.

For both men and women, local government experience is regarded as a very useful preparation for a national political career. In France, local service is seen as an important period of apprenticeship, and national deputies retain very strong local links. The same is true in Germany, where 'involvement in local politics may constitute a stepping stone to parliamentary or party positions at regional or national level'.[8] In Britain, local government experience seems to have been beneficial for female MPs: of the 83 women candidates who successfully contested elections up to 1966, 40 had served on local government bodies 'which seem to have been a useful training ground for national politics'.[9] And local government in Britain between the wars has been described as the 'front line of working-class women's advance into public life'.[10] Within the last ten years, several prominent female council leaders such as Margaret Hodge (Islington), Margaret Moran (Lewisham), Phyllis Starkey (Oxford), Beverley Hughes (Trafford) and Louise Ellman (Lancashire) have been elected to the House of Commons, whilst others such as Patricia Hollis (Norwich), Joan Hanham (Kensington and Chelsea), Emily Blatch (Cambridgeshire) and Josie Farrington (education, Lancashire) have become life peers in the House of Lords. A number of these politicians have subsequently been promoted to government positions.

Do female local politicians serve disproportionately on education, social services and welfare committees, rather than on those dealing with finance, economic planning or transport? Such evidence as we have suggests that they do, though it is not clear whether that is because they are particularly interested in such issues and feel confident about dealing with them or whether they are placed on such committees by male colleagues who themselves prefer to deal with finance, planning issues and economic development. In Britain, where the police are accountable to local police authorities which have a majority of indirectly elected councillors, plus magistrates and independent members, and on which both male and female local councillors are very keen to serve, nearly a quarter of the council representatives in 1999 were women. Of the total membership, when magistrates and independent members were included, women comprised 40 per cent. Of the 43 police authorities in England in Wales, there were only six women chairs, though it is significant, and rather exceptional as we shall see shortly, that the national Association of Police Authorities has had a six-person executive committee since its inception in 1997, composed of three men and three women.

We do have research from the Netherlands which suggests that women local politicians take a particular interest in childcare, housing matters and education. A study of women in leadership positions at regional level in Spain showed that they were usually in charge of education, culture or health and not departments of economic planning or foreign affairs. Though systematic information is not available for other countries, such evidence as we do have suggests that most of the committees chaired by women at local or regional level cover education, health, social services and welfare, areas in which women are assumed to have particular expertise based on their domestic responsibilities and experience. However, there is also some evidence from Norway and Sweden, drawn from national parliaments, that in bodies with a third and more of female members, a 'clustering effect' of women on particular committees gives way to much more equal representation across all committees. Whether that is also true for local councils and subcommittees is an issue which needs to be more fully explored.[11]

WOMEN IN LOCAL AND REGIONAL LEADERSHIP POSITIONS

To influence political agendas and to bring about significant change, women need both to win a significant proportion of local or regional council seats and to be appointed or elected to leadership positions. But right across western Europe the picture is the same – as the millennium drew to a close, there were comparatively few women who were at the head of their regional councils, local council leaders or mayors of their cities. Percentages of women who are members of local or regional executive committees are in all cases considerably lower than the percentage of women councillors. For example, in Germany in 1993, women comprised 22 per cent of local councils but only 9.6 per cent of council executive bodies. In Italy in 1990, 6.7 per cent of regional representatives were women, but they constituted only 3.5 per cent of the regional executives. In Denmark in 1994, 31 per cent of regional councillors were women but they comprised only 9.6 per cent of the executive bodies. As Britain moves towards a cabinet system for local councils, we can expect a similar pattern to emerge; the composition of those which have already been established reveals few women councillors.

If we look for female regional or provincial leaders, the situation gets even worse. In Italy in 1995, only five out of 101 provinces were led by women, and there were four female chairs of regional councils. In Ireland in 1994, out of eight regions, one was headed by a women, and in France in 1992, only one regional council out of 22 had a woman leader. In Spain in the early 1990s, only one province out of 17 had a woman at its head, and in Germany it was one region out of 16. Denmark, however, could boast three women regional presidents out of 14 regional councils.

At local level in 1993, even Denmark had fewer than 10 per cent of women council leaders – 26 out of 274 councils. In Germany it was 13 out of 203 (6.4 per cent), and in Spain 393 out of 8,046 (4.9 per cent). France had just over five per cent of women council leaders in 1989 and Italy in 1993 had 4.6 per cent. The Netherlands could boast 12.8 per cent (78 out of 608), and in Britain in 1983 the figure was 13 per cent.[12] A more up-to-date figure comes from Scotland, where in the late 1990s, 15.5 per cent of local authorities had a female leader.[13] While percentages of women elected mayors were a little higher, they were still disappointing – just under 10 per cent in Denmark, 6.7 per cent in Italy and eight per cent in France in 1999, just under 10 per cent in Spain, 12.5 per cent in Norway and 16.7 per cent in Germany. In the Netherlands, where mayors are appointed by the government, the percentage of women mayors in 1998 was 16.2 per cent, and in Sweden in the mid-1990s, the percentage of elected female mayors had reached 20 per cent.

Such evidence as we have suggests that the towns and cities which have elected women mayors are smaller rather than larger. This is certainly true in Spain, France and Italy. In France, there is only one woman mayor of a major city with a population of over 100,000, Catherine Trautmann in Strasbourg, and there are no women mayors in the large cities or metropolitan areas of Italy, and only four woman mayors out of 102 provincial towns. In Britain, the position is different. The position of mayor at the moment is a ceremonial one, and in many councils the qualification is length of council service. Thus, in the 1990s, 30 per cent of mayors were women but if there is a move to elect mayors in major cities, that percentage is likely to drop sharply on the statistical evidence we have already noted from western Europe, and particularly the finding that the larger the city, the more unlikely it is to have a female mayor.

THE IMPORTANCE OF FEMALE NETWORKS AND EQUAL OPPORTUNITY COMMITTEES

Evidence suggests that women are far less confident than men that they can represent their electors effectively at local and regional level, though their ability to do so may in fact be higher. They are also less prepared to compete for power, and may find it difficult to challenge a dominant male group in a party or council meeting. Furthermore, their domestic responsibilities may pull them away from council work, or may induce in them feelings of considerable guilt if they have to divide their time between family commitments, council committee work or municipal meetings and possibly a job as well.[14] Thus, supportive female networks have played an extremely important role in many countries in helping women to overcome the many problems facing them. At the same time, the establishment of women's committees and equal opportunity committees at local council level has enabled women councillors to take positive action to help local women's groups and to fight political, economic and social discrimination against women, thus laying the foundations for greater numbers of women to enter local and national government.

In some countries, supportive measures for women have been put in place by political parties while in other countries support networks have been provided by women's groups spanning a range of political organisations or on a non-party political basis. In Sweden, women's federations within individual political parties have played an essential role in the promotion of women in Swedish political life, and about half of women who are involved in local politics are active members of a women's federation or have passed through their party's youth federation.[15] Training is given to women to enable them to formulate their arguments, deal with male hostility or heckling and use the media effectively. Women councillors also support each other in meetings, if any one of them is the target of abuse or ridicule from male members. In Norway, similar training courses for women, designed to impart confidence in public speaking and in dealing with the media, have been organised by the main political parties for the past two decades; in recent years, the Norwegian Association of Local and Regional Authorities has operated some of them. Some of the training is specifically designed to overcome and combat 'discriminatory and hostile attitudes expressed through overt depreciation of women representatives' arguments or objections and . . . the tendency to deride . . . their opinions and embarrass them'. There have also been government-sponsored information and publicity campaigns to increase women's involvement in the political activities of local authorities, most recently in 1995. 'Local meetings and conferences were organised, advertising in leading newspapers and media was financed, publicity and information material was printed, and a national network based on one or two persons per municipality was also created . . .'.[16]

In Denmark, two broad national organisations, the National Council of Women and the Danish Women's Society have both been very active in agitating for more women in local and regional politics, by arranging meetings, producing campaign material and inviting politicians to take part in debates with their members.[17] In the Netherlands, the Association for Women in Politics was formed in 1990, based on 29 separate women's organisations, to pursue a similar strategy.[18] In France in 1992, inspired by a conference organised in Athens by the European Network 'Women in Decision Making' and the European Women's Lobby, six national women's associations joined together with the aim of encouraging women to stand in the 1995 municipal elections. They organised public meetings, mobilised potential women candidates and ensured that political leaders took measures to include them in party nominations. A different strategy emerged in the region of Alsace. Here the initiative was taken by women members of parties of the right, protesting at the lack of women candidates in the regional elections in 1992. They convened a meeting of all the women's associations in the region and it was decided to present an electoral list of women. This list gained 6.6 per cent of votes cast and sent Liliane

Gall to the regional council. She recalls that 'in the excitement, we created the *Women of Alsace* movement'. Since that time, women candidates have stood on this platform in local elections and 'two women, who were already municipal councillors, were elected as mayors . . . The *Women of Alsace* is not a political party but a people's movement.' A similar mobilisation of women's associations took place in the area of Lyon where strong women activists from both the left and right joined together to boost the numbers of women elected in the area by more than 60 per cent.[19]

In Britain, a different strategy was adopted to promote women activists and to liaise with local women's groups and feminist organisations. In 1978, Lewisham Council in London set up a women's committee, and four years later, this example was followed by the Greater London Council. Its women's committee played a prominent role in highlighting issues of concern to women, promoting women-friendly policies and working with local women's groups, and within two years, nine other London boroughs and 12 urban councils outside London had set up women's committees. Though they had only advisory status, they played an important role in drawing women into formal political activity and in establishing supportive networks at local level which helped to increase female participation in local politics. In the 1990s, women's committees have also been established in the cities of other western European countries, such as in Florence, where the 'Council of Women' includes councillors together with representatives from women's associations and groups in the city. Nantes in France has followed a slightly different course by providing the Simone de Beauvoir centre, financed by the mayor's office, where feminists and women's associations can meet and work together to co-ordinate their activities.[20] In Germany, the task of the women's councils which operate in each of the 16 federal states is to lobby Länder governments on women's issues.

A major area of activity for local councils across western Europe since the late 1970s, which has been enthusiastically promoted by women councillors, has been the development of equal opportunity policies and, where possible, new laws promoting equality. In Denmark by the mid-1990s, half the counties and about 35 municipalities had established a committee for equal opportunities or a working group to develop a policy in this area, and approximately 12 municipalities had set up a code of practice for promoting equal opportunities between the sexes in their municipal administrations. The main focus was on improving the numbers of women in top- and middle-level management positions, and then to promote men to work in the child-care sector and to join childcare education programmes. In Germany, all 16 regional governments, or Lander, have special bodies to promote equal opportunities, and nearly all have ministers for equality or for women's affairs. Several regions have passed equality laws promoting measures of 'positive action' in respect of the employment of women, and they also fund women's projects concerning education, training, employment, health care and violence against women. At local community level, there were 1,256 equality officers operating in 1992, and many of these women were instrumental in the establishment of community-based positive action plans and in funding and working with women's projects and groups. In the Netherlands, each province has a Provincial Emancipation Bureau, paid for by the provincial government, to advise the provincial government on equal opportunities issues, and at local level it is up to local communities whether or not they create a department to deal with equal opportunities. In Britain, there was a great expansion of equal opportunities departments within local authorities in the 1980s and the establishment of scores of equal opportunities committees by county and district councils. The issues discussed by one such equal opportunities committee, covering issues relating to education in Lancashire, included taking measures to increase the number of women in senior positions in schools and colleges and promoting equal curriculum and learning opportunities in schools for boys and girls.[21] Undoubtedly, such committees have helped to highlight gender discrimination in important areas of policy and to identify the series of obstacles which women have to overcome in order to rise to senior management positions.

In Ireland, a notable development in recent years has been the establishment of an Equality Subcommittee by the members of Dublin Corporation, arising from the publication of a 'Civic Charter' by a political alliance of several parties and community councillors which sought to promote equality policies in Dublin Corporation. The committee's aim is to promote gender equality at all levels including representation of councillors on committees, the promotion of women officials and the involvement of women consumers in shaping the council's policies. In Italy, almost all the regions and many of the provinces and municipalities have nominated commissions for equal opportunities, and in Spain a large number of municipalities have programmes for women and, in a few cases, a programme for the promotion of equal opportunities.[22]

DO WOMEN MAKE A DIFFERENCE?

Thus, we have outlined the problems encountered by women seeking to become local and regional councillors, and the 'clustering' of women councillors on social services, welfare and education committees. We have also seen how difficult it is for women to gain leadership positions at local and regional level, whether as members of executive or cabinet committees or as elected mayors. On the positive side, there is now considerable activity at local and regional level aimed at promoting equal opportunities for women (and also for the disabled and ethnic minorities) and at increasing their political participation. In the Scandinavian countries, and in the Netherlands and Germany, equal opportunities structures are firmly in place; in the southern countries, such as Italy, France and Spain, they are still in the process of being constructed. But there is still one question that remains difficult to answer: Do councils with a third and more of female members operate differently to more male-dominated councils? Do they have different priorities and a different political approach? We know that there are at least six councils in Denmark which have a majority of women.[23] Are there any clear differences between these councils and others with, say, only 20 per cent of women? Do they work across party lines and pursue similar political agendas? There is little research yet available on this crucial topic. We do know that in many of our countries there has been an increase in the quality and range of child-care facilities offered by local councils and the service bodies they cover; prompted no doubt by pressure from women councillors and employees. In some cases, times of meetings have been changed from evening to daytime, agendas have been shortened, and venues have been made more accessible by public transport. Equal opportunities policies have been vigorously pursued. But we need more studies which record the achievements and policy outputs of councils with a third or more of women councillors.

A further question which also needs to be asked is whether women have a different political approach to men. It has been asserted that women can change the structure and culture of politics and that women politicians tend to be more democratic and less confrontational, more open to change and to have a greater ability to work collectively than their male colleagues.[24] They are effective networkers, but prefer a team approach to working through a hierarchical structure. If all these claims are true, then local and regional councils with a third or more of women councillors should be in a strong position to establish new kinds of relationships with their local communities, and to reinvigorate local democracy. The next ten years should reveal the extent to which these hopes materialise, and should yield some detailed research based on councils with 40 per cent or more of female members which can serve as an example for those localities and regions where female councillors still constitute a quarter or less of the elected bodies.

7 The international context
Impact of the European Union and United Nations

If the 'second wave feminism' of the late 1960s and 1970s was greatly influenced by developments in the United States, the pace-setters in relation to gender equality issues over the last two decades have been the European Union and, to a lesser extent, the United Nations. Since the early 1980s, the European Union has formulated no fewer than four equal opportunity action programmes designed to put pressure on member governments and to stimulate the development of gender equality policies in member countries. At the same time, the United Nations Organisation has also organised conferences focusing on women which have highlighted the range of problems and areas of discrimination facing women across the globe. This chapter will examine the ways in which these two organisations have sought to empower women in the last two decades of the twentieth century, and will also look at the growing role of the European Parliament and of bodies such as the Council for European Municipalities and Regions and the European Women's Network in highlighting the continuation of gender inequalities in western European countries.

AIMS OF EQUALITY PROGRAMMES OF THE EU AND UN

Recent declarations by both the European Union and the United Nations Organisation leave no doubt whatever that both bodies regard the achievement of economic, social and political gender equality as fundamental to a civilised and democratic society. The European Union has made it clear in its equality programmes and equal opportunities annual reports, published since 1996, that the under-representation of women constitutes a serious loss for society as a whole and does not allow the interests and needs of the whole population to be catered for in full. It results in a democratic deficit, a serious loss of talent and expertise and a failure to engage with women's concerns and needs. Thus, the European Commission regards it as essential for the democratic development and legitimacy of existing governments and their institutions that women are treated fairly and equally and are enabled to play a full part in social, economic and political life. There are concerns that if women's values and life circumstances are not taken into consideration by decision makers, women will increasingly fail to identify with the prevailing political system, and that if their continuing underrepresentation in politics is not addressed as a matter of urgency, the democratic development, cohesion and competitiveness of the European Union will suffer.[1]

The fourth United Nations world conference on the status of women, held in Beijing in 1995, adopted a comprehensive and wide-ranging Platform for Action to set an agenda for 'women's empowerment'. Its slogan was 'Half of the world – half of the power', and it declared that 'without the active participation of women and incorporation of women's perspective at all levels of decision-making, the goals of equality, development and peace cannot be achieved'. It also stated that women in politics and in decision-making positions would contribute to redefining political priorities, would place new items on political agendas which reflected and addressed women's gender-specific concerns, values and experiences, and would provide new perspectives on mainstream political issues. Thus, balanced participation of the sexes would give rise to 'different ideals, values and behaviour' which would result in more justice and equality in the world for both men and women.[2]

Both the European Union and the United Nations Organisation have therefore put much effort in recent years into establishing frameworks for action in the field of gender equality, and as we shall see, this work is ongoing. The rationale for empowerment and for equality is clear and compelling, but the difficulty has been to transform fine words into concrete actions and policies at national, regional and local level.

THE EU ACTION PROGRAMMES CONCERNING WOMEN

The European Union's policies relating to women have broadened considerably since the original statement in Article 119 of the Treaty of Rome that men and women should receive equal pay. In the 1970s, three equality directives were passed, in 1975, 1976 and 1979, covering equal pay, equal treatment in employment and equal treatment in social security matters. To implement, monitor and review these directives, a women's information bureau and women's employment bureau were established within the European Commission and the existing equal pay unit was expanded. A permanent advisory commission on equal opportunities was set up, and this commission drafted a new action programme on equal opportunities, which was submitted to the council in 1981.[3]

In 1982, this action programme was adopted as the first European Union Community Action Programme on the Promotion of Equal Opportunities for Women. The programme focused on issues of equal pay, equal rights for access to employment and vocational training, equality of working conditions and the importance of social protection. The aim of the programme, which ran from 1982 to 1985, was to stimulate further measures in member states, by funding a range of positive action and pilot projects. This was followed in 1986 by a second Medium-term Community Programme for Women, which ran from 1986 to 1990. This programme built on the first, and implemented directives on equality in an enlarged community of 12 member states. It extended the scope of equal opportunities into new spheres of positive action in training, new technology, policies to harmonise working and family life and local development. These directives were particularly effective in countries aspiring to European Union membership, such as Spain, which joined the European Community in 1986.

A major element of the third Medium-term Community Action Programme on Equal Opportunities for Women and Men, to run from 1991 to 1995, was the introduction of the concept of 'mainstreaming'. In the 1990s, equal opportunities was to become a mainstream policy, an essential ingredient in all European Union policies, to be applied alongside more specific positive actions. 'Mainstreaming' called for the 'development of a gender perspective and gender analysis of all policies, programmes and actions' adopted by the European Union,[4] and sought to ensure that women were involved in the decision-making processes related to policy development. As a result of the introduction of mainstreaming, efforts were devoted to promoting equal opportunities for women and men through Structural Fund programmes, and in all the Community programmes in the fields of education, training and youth. Equally importantly, the issue of women's participation in decision making was identified as a policy issue. Data began to be collected more systematically on the numbers of women active in the political process at European, national, regional and local levels in member states, and awareness campaigns were organised to increase the numbers of women elected as political representatives, resulting, for example, in an increased number of women MEPs elected to the European Parliament in 1994.[5]

An important move by the Commission under the aegis of the third Action Programme was the establishment of the European Network of Experts on Women in Decision Making. This network, comprising one expert from each member state, had a threefold remit, to gather and analyse data relating to women's participation in politics in member states, to organise conferences and to disseminate information on the status of women in decision making in the European Union. Together with the European Women's Lobby, a coalition of non-governmental women's groups across the European Union, founded in 1990, it organised a European Summit and conference on 'Women in Power' in Athens in October 1992. The resulting Athens Declaration, signed by those present, including women ministers from member states, called attention to the prevailing 'profound inequality in all public and political decision-making authorities and bodies at every level – local, regional, national and European', proclaimed the need to achieve a balanced distribution of public and political power between women and men and called for the establishment of a specific policy to redress the democratic deficit. This conference was followed four years later by the Rome Summit 'Women for the Renewal of Politics and Society', held in May 1996 and organised jointly by the Italian presidency and the Commission. At this conference, women ministers from member states of the European Union signed the Charter of Rome, committing their governments to work to achieve a gender balance in decision making. The Charter called for the balanced participation of women and men in decision-making positions, declared the issue of equality to be a priority for the Union and stressed the necessity for concrete action at all levels to promote the equal participation of women and men in decision making in all spheres of society. In 1999, a further conference, organised at the request of Martine Aubry, the French Minister for Employment, with the support of the Commission, was held in Paris to discuss ways of combating the continuing under-representation of women in decision-making processes. In his closing speech to the conference, the French Prime Minister Lionel Jospin stressed the democratic deficit arising from the underrepresentation of women and drew attention to a national action plan to be introduced in 2000 by the French government on equal opportunities in all areas of political, economic, professional and social life.[6]

In addition to organising conferences, the European Network of Experts on 'Women in Decision-making' has published data on the level of women's participation in decision making across the European Union and organised a conference in Dublin in March 1995 to discuss strategies to achieve a gender balance in political decision making. The conference resulted in a guide for the implementation of policies geared to increasing the participation of women in political decision making, and a brochure on 'Facts and Figures on Women in Political and Public Decision Making in Europe' published in 11 languages.[7]

The first three action programmes were implemented on the initiative of the European Commission, but the fourth Medium Term Community Action Programme on Equal Opportunities for Women and Men (1996–2000) was proposed by the European Commission to the Council, and subsequently established by a Council of Ministers decision. The principle of mainstreaming was emphasised even more firmly, when it was agreed that equal opportunities for women and men were to be incorporated as a central element into all European Community policies and activities. The Council decision laying down the fourth Action Programme outlined five further policy aims, in addition to mainstreaming: mobilising all actors to achieve equality, promoting equality in a changing economy, reconciling work and family life, promoting a gender balance in decision making and creating optimum conditions for the exercise of equality rights. The projects under the fourth Action Programme were designed to spread good practice, pool information and experience, build on existing networks, collect and disseminate data and encourage leadership training. An important initiative was the establishment of the FrauenComputer-Zentrum in Berlin, designed to exploit the capacity of new information technology to build up a database of information concerned with women in decision making. Launched on the Internet in January 1998, the principal aim of this project was to make women decision-makers more visible, to identify areas where women have not yet reached higher levels as a starting-point for strategies to promote equal representation and to promote a gender balance in decision making through contacts made in collecting the data and through subsequent dissemination.[8]

In 1997, the Amsterdam Treaty was agreed, emphasising in Article 2 the principle of equality between women and men, and assigning to the Community in Article 3 the duty to eliminate inequalities and to promote equality in all its activities. Article 13 of the Treaty will enable action to be taken to combat all discrimination, including that based on sex or sexual orientation. Thus, the Treaty specifically identified the elimination of inequality between women and men and the promotion of equality in all the European Union's activities as being amongst its fundamental aims. The agreement to strengthen and mainstream equal opportunities policies at European level has been a major factor in raising the political profile of women's right to equality, and in addition to adopting Action Programmes designed to galvanise member states into adopting gender equality policies, the European Commission has also launched three Action Programmes to address a serious underrepresentation of women in management positions in the European Commission itself. The first positive Action Programme was launched in March 1988, and included measures relating to recruitment, career development, training and increasing awareness. A second programme was followed, in 1997, by a Third Action Programme for Equal Opportunities for Women and Men at the Commission, aimed at designing a strategy 'for achieving balanced participation by women and men in the decision-making process in each institution, subsidiary body and decentralised body of the European Community'. Some 46 per cent of the Commission staff in 1997 were women, and the percentage in the most senior posts, category A, increased from 11.5 per cent in 1992 to 17.5 per cent by 1996.[9] Recruitment and promotion targets were fixed in 1998 for senior grades, including the nomination of women to director grade, the increase of nominations to middle management level and the recruitment of a maximum number of women at principal administrative level. These objectives were carefully monitored by an Equal Opportunities Unit and had been partially met by September 1998.[10]

WOMEN COMMISSIONERS

One visible sign of women in senior positions in the European Union is the number of women commissioners. Between 1994 and 1999, out of 20 commissioners, chosen by their respective member states, five were women, as against only two out of 17 between 1989 and 1993. The oldest commissioner, Anita Gradin from Sweden, was given responsibility for immigration, home affairs and justice while Ritt Bjerregaard from Denmark covered environmental issues. Monika Wulf-Mathies from Germany dealt with regional policy, while Emma Bonino from Italy had the fisheries and consumer affairs portfolios. The fifth female commissioner, former French Prime Minister Edith Cresson, oversaw education, training and youth programmes and was heavily criticised in 1999, along with Wulf-Mathies, in a report into corruption in the Commission.

None the less, the incoming European Commission President in 1999, Romano Prodi, was under great pressure to ensure that the new European Commission contained at least five women, and after a number of sensitive negotiations with member states, this target was reached. The new women commissioners have been given port- folios covering transport and energy, social policy, education and culture, the budget and the environment, and they include a Spanish lawyer and former Agricultural Minister, Loyola de Palacio, a German member of the Green Party and briefly a Minister for the Environment in Berlin, Michele Schrcyer, and a Swedish Social Demo- crat and former Minister for Health and Social Affairs, Margot Wallstrom.[11]

THE ROLE OF THE EUROPEAN PARLIAMENT

Before 1979, members of the European Parliament were nominated by member states, and just before the elections of June 1979 there were only 12 women out of a total of 198. Interestingly, the first direct elec- tions in 1979 produced a considerable rise – from 6 per cent to 16 per cent – in the level of female representation. In Britain, Italy, Ireland, Denmark and the Netherlands, the percentage of women elected was greater than at national level, and in France 22 per cent of women were elected to the European Parliament as against only 5 per cent to the National Assembly. Though there has been little research into the reasons for the higher percentage of female representatives elected to the European Parliament, one possible explanation is that the competi- tion for seats may have been less intense than at national level, and as a result selection processes may have been more open. In addition, in France, voting was by proportional representation rather than by the two-ballot system in individual constituencies used at national level (see Chapter 8).

Since 1979, the numbers of women MEPs have risen steadily. In 1984, they made up 17 per cent of the parliament, but this percentage had risen to 26.4 per cent by 1994, even before the accession in 1995 of Sweden, Finland and Austria. The figures from individual political parties reveal that more women were elected from parties of the left and centre than from those of the right. In 1979, only 8 per cent of the 108-strong European People's Party delegation (mainly Christian

Table 6 Results of the European Elections, 1999

	Total	Women MEPs	% Women MEPs
Sweden	22	11	50.0
Finland	16	7	43.8
France	87	35	40.2
Austria	21	8	38.1
Denmark	16	6	37.5
Germany	99	36	37.4
Netherlands	31	10	35.5
Spain	64	22	34.4
Ireland	15	5	33.3
Belgium	25	7	32.0
UK	87	21	24.1
Portugal	25	5	20.0
Greece	25	4	16.0
Italy	87	10	11.5
Luxembourg	6	0	0.0
Total	*626*	*187*	*30.0*

Source: European Commission, *Women of Europe* newsletter, July/Aug. 1999

Democrat Parties) were women, compared to over 20 per cent of the communist, socialist and liberal delegations and this difference was still apparent in the delegations of the 1994–99 parliament. It is, however, interesting to note that despite the swing to the right in many member states in the elections of June 1999, the overall percentage of women again increased – to 30 per cent, and included some surprisingly high numbers of women elected from France, Spain and Ireland.

A number of factors combined to produce this further increase in women's representation. The two leading countries in the table in terms of women's representation, Sweden and Finland, joined the European Union after the 1994 elections, and since their accession have campaigned vigorously in the Council of Ministers, the Commission and the European Parliament on a range of equality issues. In addition, women's networks, of the kind we noted in Chapter 6, were very active in campaigning for more women to be included on party lists in winnable positions. Most political parties themselves were keen to demonstrate their commitment to equality and to underline their wide range of candidates and broad appeal to all sections of the electorate by including a number of women amongst their candidates and putting them in winnable positions in party lists.

A handful of women have played prominent roles in the European Parliament since 1979. The French minister Simone Weil was the first president of the directly elected parliament in 1979, though it took another 20 years for a second woman, Nicole Fontaine, also French, to be elected to that position. In the 1994–99 parliament, Christa Randzio-Plath from Germany chaired a sub-committee on monetary affairs and Pauline Green from Britain led the largest political group in the parliament, the 200-strong Party of European Socialists (PES). There were three female vice-presidents out of 14, including the German MEP Ursula Schleicher and three out of 20 women presidents of standing committees.[12] Laura Alvarcz from Spain was a vice-president of the Confederal Group of the European United Left/Nordic Green Left. Alongside the parliament, in 1998, Beatrice Machiavelli from Italy was elected president of the influential Economic and Social Committee.

However, the women members of the European Parliament have exercised considerably more influence through assiduous networking across national and party groupings and particularly through the Committee on Women's Rights. The first directly elected parliament in 1979 set up an *ad hoc* committee under the chairmanship of Yvette Roudy of France to examine the position of women in the European Community. The result of many months of hard work was the adoption of a resolution in February 1981 detailing the specific problems and discrimination experienced by women across member states. In the summer of that year, the parliament set up a committee of enquiry to review the extent to which the objectives in the resolution, aimed at improving the situation facing women, were being achieved and to monitor developments. Some two and a half years later, this committee of inquiry submitted a report and a motion for a resolution which was adopted in January 1994. Its 116 articles provided a clear framework for a policy on women, and also provided the impetus for the establishment of a permanent committee on women's rights by the new parliament, elected in 1984.

Since the mid-1980s, the Committee on Women's Rights has been extremely active in monitoring the application of directives in force in the area of equal opportunities and considering policies in the field of education, vocational training, new technologies and employment. It has drawn up numerous reports and, in the 1994–9 parliament, focused its activities on ensuring that equal opportunities between women and men were incorporated into all Community actions and policies whilst at the same time supporting measures of positive action to promote women in areas where they were particularly disadvantaged.[13] Other European organisations such as the Congress of Local and Regional Authorities of Europe and the Council of European Municipalities and Regions have also organised conferences and carried out research into the continuing underrepresentation of women in the cities and regions of Europe, helping to provide more data about the inequalities and problems still being faced by women in the European Union and discussing their findings with members of the European Parliament and the Committee on Women's Rights.[14]

OTHER EUROPEAN BODIES

It is interesting to note that the percentages of women on two appointed European Union bodies, the Economic and Social Committee and the Committee of the Regions, are considerably lower than that of the European Parliament. The 222 members of the Economic and Social Committee are nominated by member state governments every four years and represent employers, workers and 'other interests'. Only 13 per cent of its membership was female between 1994 and 1998, though this percentage rose to 17 per cent in the committee appointed to serve from 1998 to 2002. The Committee of the Regions, established under the Treaty of Maastricht to provide a forum for representatives of local and regional government in the European Union, only had 22 women appointees out of a total of 222 in its first term of office from 1994–98, though nearly double that number were amongst the alternate delegates appointed. In its second term of office, the numbers of women appointed rose to 33, or nearly 15 per cent, with over 21 per cent of women alternates. None the less, these figures are considerably lower than one might expect, taking into account the percentages of women elected at regional and local level in member states and the number of women MEPs. One explanation must be that leadership positions at local and regional government level, from which members of the Committee of the Regions are drawn, are still heavily occupied by men, as noted in Chapter 6, and a second factor is likely to be keen competition within member states for places on the Committee of the Regions.[15]

THE UNITED NATIONS AND WOMEN

In addition to the activities of the European Union, the United Nations has also worked to promote equal opportunities and women' rights across the globe. The first United Nations World Conference on Women was held in Mexico City in 1975, and was followed by the United Nations Decade for Women: Equality, Development and Peace, which was aimed at encouraging national governments to take action and frame policies to extend women's rights and opportunities. The conference in Mexico City was followed in 1980 by a second conference in Copenhagen and a third, five years later, in Nairobi. At Nairobi, 'Forward looking strategies for the advancement of women to the year 2000' were adopted, based on recommendations for action designed to improve the position of women throughout the world.

Though these United Nations conferences undoubtedly contributed to an increase in awareness and discussion of women's issues, they did not stimulate much concrete economic or political change. As a result, it was agreed that there should be another world conference to review progress since 1985 and to set out new commitments and strategies for the future, and this took place in Beijing in 1995. It was preceded by five regional preparatory conferences organised by the respective United Nations regional commissions, and the relevant meeting which covered Europe, as well as North America and Israel, was held in Vienna in October 1994. The priorities identified by this region were the promotion of women's human rights, the alleviation of women's poverty, the promotion of women's contribution to the economy, equality of treatment of female and male workers and reconciliation of work and family life, gender-specific statistics and research and the increased participation of women in public life.

At the Beijing conference, an ambitious and wide-ranging Platform for Action was adopted, including sections on women and the economy and women in power and decision making. A section on women and the environment called for women's active participation in policy making affecting the environment and the insertion of a gender perspective into such policy making and programmes, and there was also a call for the elimination of discrimination and negative attitudes against girl children in families and in education and training, inheritance and the labour market. The Beijing conference was 'the largest body of people ever gathered together to reach agreement on a Platform for Action addressing the most pressing equality issues on a global level' and gave a rousing reception to one of the closing speeches of the conference, given by the Prime Minister of Norway, Gro Harlem Brundtland. She declared that the conference would 'irrevocably shape world opinion' in spite of a continuing 'genderised apartheid' and called on delegates to return to their countries 'to change values and attitudes' in 'boardrooms, . . . suburbia, . . . local communities, . . . governments' and at United Nations headquarters.[16]

Member states of the European Union outlined their plans to meet the goals identified in the Platform for Action in follow-up reports published the following year. Meanwhile, the Council of Ministers agreed to review the EU's implementation of the Platform on an annual basis, and a follow-up conference was held in Spain in November 1995 to discuss how to transform commitments into practical policies in the areas of decision making, mainstreaming equal opportunities and the image of women in society. The United Nations Committee on the Status of Women, meeting in New York in 1997, provided a further opportunity to network with government representatives and members and employees of international organisations to discuss ways of implementing the policies identified in the Platform for Action. This body has proved invaluable in taking forward the issues identified at Beijing, and in making preparations for a United Nations General Assembly Special Session on Women which took place in 2000 on the themes of gender equality, development and peace for the twenty-first century.[17] Women's groups throughout Europe, in addition to the official relevant organisations within the European Union, have been busily preparing papers and position statements for this gathering, which will undoubtedly give a further stimulus to governments to show positive results in the area of equal opportunities policies.

Thus, the 1980s and 1990s have seen considerable activity by the European Union and the United Nations to highlight the continuing discrimination and underrepresentation experienced by women and to pressurise governments into adopting policies to promote gender equality. While the two bodies can only construct frameworks for action and exhort member states to turn words into action, their continuing efforts to monitor the progress of conference declarations and the implementation of action programmes have undoubtedly had a considerable impact in promoting awareness of the persistence of the many obstacles which women still face in their professional, political and personal lives. They have also played a major part in constructing strategies for positive action, and in persuading governments to implement them, thus underlining the growing importance of the influence of international bodies at the beginning of a new millennium.

8   Electoral systems

One factor which has regularly been identified as a crucial 'enabling condition' for women to progress within a political system is the type of electoral system used. For example, a study by Norris found that although cultural attitudes were significant in shaping women's representation, institutional factors were the most significant, notably whether a system of proportional representation was in operation.[1] Almost a decade later, Rule and Zimmerman were able to claim that almost 30 per cent of the varying proportion of women in national legislatures could be accounted for by electoral systems. They claimed that 'several studies document that the system for selecting MPs is the single most important predictor of women's recruitment to parliament'.[2]

In their world-wide study, Rule and Zimmerman found that between 1987 and 1991, the 17 countries using a system of proportional representation or party lists had proportions of women in their parliaments which were approximately double that in the eight countries using non-proportional systems. The first group of countries, including Scandinavia but also Spain, Italy and Greece, had an average of almost 20 per cent women in parliament, compared with less than 10 per cent in the second group, which included Britain and the United States. What can explain this clear pattern? There seem to be two interrelating factors which are important: first, the broad type of electoral system used, but second, the total number of MPs elected within each constituency or district. Before exploring in detail why the number of women elected may be related to these two connected factors, it is necessary to briefly describe the three main types of electoral system used in our ten countries.

TYPES OF ELECTORAL SYSTEM

Perhaps the simplest form of electoral system is that found in Britain, the plurality system. The country is divided into a number of individual constituencies, which each elect a single representative (in parliamentary elections) or occasionally two or three representatives (in some local elections[3]). The voter has as many votes as there are places to be filled, and the candidate(s) with the most votes is elected. This electoral system is not used in Europe outside the United Kingdom, but is common in countries once within the British Empire, such as the United States, Canada and India. The second type of electoral systems are majority systems, where the winning candidate requires over half of the votes cast to be elected. This system is also based on single-member districts, but either requires second preferences of the third-placed and lower candidates to be taken into account (the 'alternative vote' as used in Australia), or a second ballot or 'run-off' between the two leading candidates from the first ballot, the system generally used in France under the present Fifth Republic.[4]

The third type of electoral system, proportional representation, can come in an almost inexhaustible number of forms. The common feature is that seats are allocated in broad proportion to the overall number of votes cast, which recognises the existence of nationally or regionally-based political parties and necessitates the use of multi-member constituencies or districts. Generally each party will put up a list of candidates for each district, and will gain a number of seats in relation to the votes cast. These seats will either be filled automatically from the top of the party list down ('closed list' systems) or alternatively voters may be allowed to overturn the order of the party list by casting preference votes ('open list' systems). The other factor which can vary is the size of the multi-member districts being used; at one end of the scale the entire country can form a single district, as in the Netherlands. More common is for multi-member districts to be based on regions, electing perhaps seven to eleven members each (see Table 7). At the other end of the scale (usually in smaller countries), multi-member districts may elect only three or four representatives, which is the case under Ireland's 'single transferable vote' system.[5] As a general rule, the fewer the number of representatives elected in each district, the less proportional the system.

Two of the countries in our study, Germany and Italy, have chosen to combine two of the above categories in a single electoral system for parliamentary elections. The plurality system is used to elect a number of representatives in individual constituencies, but a number of MPs are also elected from national party lists to ensure the overall result is proportional. Germany (and previously West Germany) has used this 'additional member' system throughout the post-war period, allowing a number of studies to be made comparing the outcomes of the two 'parts' of the mixed system. Italy only moved to a mixed electoral system in the 1990s, having previously used a wholly proportional system before the reforms of 1993.

ELECTORAL SYSTEMS AND WOMEN IN PARLIAMENT

Table 7 lists the ten countries in our study, detailing the broad electoral system used in each, the average number of MPs elected per district, and the number of women in parliament at the most recent general election. The finding by Rule and others that women are helped by proportional electoral systems is backed up by the data in our ten countries; the six which use wholly proportional systems have an average of 31 per cent women in their parliaments compared with an

Table 7 Electoral systems and women in parliament in the ten countries

Country	Electoral system	MPs per district (average)	Total MPs	Women MPs	% Women	Year
Sweden	Proportional	11	349	149	42.7	1998
Denmark	Proportional	8	179	67	37.4	1998
Norway	Proportional	8	165	60	36.4	1997
Netherlands	Proportional	National	150	54	36.0	1998
Germany	Mixed	*	669	207	30.9	1998
Spain	Proportional	7	348	75	21.6	1996
UK	Plurality	1	659	121	18.4	1997
Ireland	Proportional	4	166	20	12.0	1997
Italy	Mixed	*	630	70	11.1	1996
France	Majority (2 ballot)	1	577	63	10.9	1997

Sources: The average size of multi-member districts are calculated from D. Leonard and R. Natkiel, *World Atlas of Elections* (The Economist Publications, 1986). Data on numbers of women are derived from the website of the Inter-Parliamentary Union and relate to the most recent parliamentary election.

Note: * The German and Italian electoral systems are based on a mix of proportional and plurality elements. Approximately half the members of the German Bundestag are elected in individual constituencies, the other half from national party lists. In Italy, the proportions are approximately 75:25 per cent.

average of 21 per cent in the two countries with mixed systems and just 14.6 per cent in the two elected by plurality or majority systems.

The wide differential in proportions of women elected by each type of electoral system is the first of two clear patterns emerging from Table 7. The second is that the percentage of women elected seems to drop as the number of representatives elected by each constituency decreases. At the extreme end of the scale are the non-proportional systems which elect only one representative per constituency, such as France and the UK, which have historically suffered from extremely low levels of women's representation. Indeed these two countries still had comparatively low proportions of women elected in 1997, despite the introduction of quotas by the French Socialists and British Labour Party (see Chapter 4). Proportional systems may use large districts (as in Sweden and the Netherlands) or small districts (as in Ireland). What seems clear is that systems which use large multi-member constituencies are more likely to facilitate the entry of women into parliament. Not only does Sweden with an average 11 members per district enjoy the highest proportion of women parliamentarians in the world, but the Netherlands, with just one multi-member district covering the entire country, has the highest proportion of women MPs in the world outside Scandinavia. Ireland may have a highly proportional electoral system, but the small number of members elected per district seems not to facilitate the election of nearly as many women to parliament as other proportional systems. Indeed, Bystydzienski states that 'it is usually essential that the number of representatives per district be five or more for the election of women in meaningful numbers'.[6]

Why should this be so? Why is it that countries using single-member districts tend to elect few women, while countries with large multi-member districts tend to enjoy a much more even gender balance? The explanation may well relate back to the selection process of political parties. Simply put, where a party selects a single candidate, they are likely to choose a man, since as a general rule a male seems 'safe' as a candidate while a woman may appear 'risky'. More specific reasons behind such prejudices are the belief that voters are less likely to vote for a woman than a man (an assertion for which in Britain at least there is no evidence whatsoever), that men fulfil traditional stereotypes of what a typical parliamentarian should look like and that they are more likely to enjoy the necessary qualities which appeal to a party selectorate (see Chapter 4). However, where a party is required to draw up a list of several candidates, they will include a balance of men and women, because of the need to appeal to as many voters as possible. This is particularly the case where lists are drawn up on a national basis. If a local party draws up a list of, for example, two or three names for a small multi-member district, they may still both be men, particularly if there is a need to represent other divides such as geographical parts of a constituency or different party factions.

Again looking at the data in our ten countries, it is noteworthy that the Swedish Social Democrats elected on average over five representatives per constituency in 1985. In only one of 28 districts did the party win less than three seats. In Norway, the Labour Party elected on average nearly four representatives per constituency in their election held the same month, with three or more MPs elected in 16 of 19 districts. By contrast, in Ireland it has been highly unusual for even the two biggest parties to win three or more seats in any district.[7] In 1982, both Fianna Fáil and Fine Gael averaged less than two representatives per constituency, and there were only six individual instances of a party winning as many as three MPs in a single district. This variation in the numbers of MPs elected by party in each constituency may go a long way to explaining the varying levels of women's representation apparent in Table 7. In Sweden and Norway, the large parties are likely to include some women in a four- or five-person delegation to parliament, even if all constituency lists are still headed by a man. As Bystydzienski states, 'when several persons can represent a party in one constituency, female candidates are not the party's only representatives within a given election unit and thus have a better chance of being nominated and elected'.[8] In Ireland (or indeed the UK), where a party's representation in each constituency is only one or two persons strong, that representation is overwhelmingly likely to be made up entirely of men.

COUNTRIES USING MORE THAN ONE ELECTORAL SYSTEM

Evidence from countries using a combination of electoral systems strongly reinforces the view that the type of electoral system used plays a crucial role in shaping the proportion of women elected. Perhaps the best example is Germany, where half of the representatives elected to the Bundestag represent individual constituencies, while the other half are elected from national party lists. The mixed or 'additional member' electoral system therefore combines the two extreme cases discussed above: for individual constituencies each party will select a single candidate, while the party will draw up a list of perhaps

100 to 200 candidates for the proportional half of the system. Needless to say, the proportion of women elected has been substantially lower in individual constituencies than from the national lists. In 1990, for example, only 39 women were elected in the 328 constituency seats (12 per cent), while 93 were elected from party lists (28 per cent).[9] This pattern was partially accounted for by the tendency of smaller more 'women-friendly' parties, such as the Greens and former Communists, to mainly win list seats, but there was also a clear discrepancy within the representation of both the Social Democrats and Christian Democrats, with double the proportion of women elected from party lists as compared with individual constituencies. Interestingly, this 2:1 ratio of women elected by the proportional as compared with the plurality element is almost identical to that calculated by Rule and Zimmerman (see note 6, this chapter) for all democracies across the world.

Evidence from other countries is based on the use of different electoral systems for different elections. Of course other factors may be important here as well as the type of electoral system used, but the findings do tend in a similar direction. For example, the UK moved to various systems of proportional representation in 1999 for elections to the European Parliament, Scottish Parliament and Welsh Assembly. In all cases the number of women elected exceeded the proportion of 18 per cent holding seats in the national parliament. The fact that there is also a higher proportion of women councillors in Britain than there are female MPs (see Chapter 6) may also relate to the electoral system, since in local elections, the use of multi-member constituencies under a plurality system often leads to two or three candidates from the same party being elected at the same time, which may encourage the selection of women. Even greater differentials are apparent in France, which has elected a far higher proportion of women to the European Parliament using a proportional list system than to its own National Assembly by the single-member majority system. In 1984, almost 20 per cent of French MEPs were women, compared with approximately 5 per cent of French MPs. By 1999, the proportion of MEPs exceeded 40 per cent, while women's representation in parliament was just 11 per cent. It should be noted that a short-lived change in the parliamentary electoral system to proportional representation in 1986 did not lead to a significant increase in the numbers of women elected. The proportion of women only increased from 5.3 to 5.9 per cent, with most women placed well down their respective party lists, perhaps because women failed to react to the change quickly enough to press the case for more women candidates.[10] This proved an important exception to the general rule, as it showed that a proportional electoral system may be necessary for women to gain election in significant numbers, but the system does not itself guarantee such an outcome.

PREFERENCE VOTING

As outlined in our introduction to different types of electoral systems, some proportional systems allow voters to change the order of a party list by casting 'preference votes'. Has this practice helped or hindered women? The balance of opinion has been that, despite the potential benefit to women, preferential voting has tended to be a disadvantage for women candidates. In the Italian electoral system before 1993, preference votes could often be important given the fragmented and factionalised nature of party politics. However, most women candidates lacked the necessary 'personal capital' such as a prestigious position in society or a charismatic personality, or indeed the access to favours which were such a key part of the Italian political system before the scandals of the early 1990s. As a result, women tended to collect fewer preference votes than men.[11] In Norway, preference voting, including the power to cross names out, add them to the list or even give a candidate an extra vote, has been permitted in local elections, and was used to boost the representation of women in high profile campaigns in 1967 and 1971. However, in general, preference voting has not worked to the advantage of women, and may be one reason why female representation is lower at local than regional level.[12]

ARE ELECTORAL SYSTEMS SIMPLY A PRODUCT OF WIDER POLITICAL CULTURE?

To end this chapter, we should perhaps reflect that electoral systems were not designed in a political vacuum, and may simply be the product of the prevalent political culture within each country. Thus, the fact that electoral systems in the Scandinavian countries are highly proportional may reflect an inclusive political culture, where all sections of society and new political groups are encouraged to become a part of the political system. The use of a proportional system in large multi-member constituencies enables all significant groups to be represented in parliament, whether left-wing socialists, communists or indeed women. It could be argued that this desire for inclusion may be an important reason why the electoral system developed in its current form.

By contrast, it could be argued that the cautious evolution of the electoral system in Britain has reflected a traditionally 'closed' society where all new groups, whether women, environmentalists or extreme parties, are discouraged from entering the political system. For example, it was in Britain that the record vote for a Green Party was recorded (15 per cent in the 1989 European elections), yet the plurality electoral system kept them out of the political system, rewarding them with no representatives rather than the double-figure delegation they would have enjoyed under a proportional system. The same fate has in the past kept the extreme left and right out of the British political system, with many arguing such exclusion to be a positive virtue of the electoral system. Thus, the form of electoral system which is in use may not be accidental; its outcomes are likely to be those which appeal to the dominant forces in society. As a result the fact that so much of the variation in the number of women elected to national parliaments appears to be explained by the electoral system alone may not get us as far as we would like. We still need to ask why is it that Britain and France have resisted a move to proportional systems for their national parliaments? If a desire for an exclusive rather than an inclusive political system looms large in the explanation, then the choice of electoral system becomes merely a means to an end, simply a proxy for the prevailing closed political culture, which by definition would aim to keep women out of the political system.

9 Conclusion

Do women make a difference?

The advance of women through the political system has been one of the most significant developments of the second half of the twentieth century. For the first time we have seen women prime ministers and presidents. The proportion of women members of parliament in our ten countries has increased from just 5.8 per cent in 1945 to over 25 per cent by the end of 1997, and the percentage of women in national governments has increased from a derisory level to 28 per cent over the same period. The number of women involved in political decision making accelerated in a number of countries as we reached the end of the twentieth century, and the goal of 'parity' between women and men no longer appears an impossible dream.

But does the increased participation of women in decision-making positions make a difference? Has the political agenda been altered or the style of politics changed? At present, available studies are surprisingly scarce and inconclusive. Even in one of our Scandinavian countries, Denmark, a recent paper claimed that 'there is not the necessary empirical material to answer this question'.[1] At the top of the political system, numbers of women leaders have been so small that the absence of detailed studies of their behaviour is perhaps unsurprising. However, there have been a handful of studies of women parliamentarians, particularly in Britain and Norway, and their findings will be referred to. Given the accelerating numbers of women in parliament over the last 10 to 20 years (see Table 8), one would expect the number of detailed studies to increase significantly in the next few years, increasing our understanding of the ways in which women have or have not changed politics.

In the absence of large numbers of detailed studies, the best way of approaching the question of what difference women in power make is to ask what the political system lacks when women are excluded or underrepresented. Once we can see what a political system lacks without women, we can assess the difference the presence of women might be expected to make, or indeed whether we could expect women to make any significant difference. Before we do that, however, it is necessary to review a number of theories on women and power, which have implications for our discussion on whether women make a difference. Broadly, these theories divide into 'optimistic' and 'pessimistic' viewpoints. It is particularly important for the optimistic theories that women do demonstrate a real difference; the pessimistic hypotheses assume that women will never achieve real power, and as a result will never be in a position to make a difference.

THEORIES ON WOMEN AND POWER

Many theories on women and power were initially developed in Scandinavian countries to explain the lack of women's progress in the 1970s, but new theories have been developed in light of the numerical advances made by women in the 1980s and 1990s. Two theories suggest that we might expect the disadvantages faced by women to disappear over time, but ranged against them are a variety of 'iron laws' which suggest that women will always be relegated to secondary roles. The first such theory points to the continued absence of women from leading political positions, a pattern of *hierarchical marginalisation*. Women remain confined to traditional roles, with responsibility for 'reproductive' issues, while men retain a near monopoly of leadership positions and other positions regarded as powerful, such as control of financial ministries. A second hypothesis is that of *shrinking institutions*, which suggests that as women move into positions of political leadership, those positions are simultaneously becoming less important. Real power is shifting away from formal political positions to a growing informal 'corporate' world, to supra-national bodies, to growing financial institutions and to powerful multinational companies. Needless to say, these organisations remain totally dominated by men.

Such 'iron laws' are open to challenge on the basis that the 1980s and 1990s have seen a significant increase in the numbers of women in government, including the emergence of a number of women leaders and others in positions of real power. For example, it would be difficult to maintain that Margaret Thatcher did not wield large amounts of power. Indeed, it is commonly argued that the position of British prime minister became more powerful than ever during her period in office. In addition, women in government are no longer confined to 'reproductive' ministries such as education, health and welfare, as

Chapter 5 has already demonstrated. None the less, the same chapter did note the continued male dominance in the very top government positions, and the continued absence of women from other key policy areas, notably finance, foreign affairs and defence. Finally, it is undoubtedly the case that national governments are losing some power to supra-national bodies such as the European Union but, as outlined in Chapter 7, the EU has taken a leading role in formulating women-friendly policies since the 1970s.

To counter the pessimistic 'iron laws of power' hypothesis, two alternative theories have been developed. The first optimistic view is the *time-lag hypothesis*, which suggests that the political marginalisation of women will slowly diminish as women become established within the political system.[2] Such a development would mirror that of, for example, working-class parties which initially struggled to break into government at the turn of the century, but began to succeed several decades after their formation. Thus, in the twenty-first century we might expect the remaining 'male bastions' slowly to crumble, and the number of women leaders to increase. The unprecedented election of a woman, Michèle Alliot-Marie, to head the French Gaullist Party in late 1999 may be a sign of things to come; a woman filling such a key position may become the norm in the twenty-first century.

The second 'optimistic' viewpoint is the *critical mass theory* developed by Dahlerup and others, which suggests that women will make a difference, but only when present in sufficient numbers, perhaps 30 per cent or 40 per cent of an elected body.[3] In small numbers, women cannot be expected to alter conventions which have developed over many years, and on a second level they themselves will be expected to conform to existing norms if they wish to be accepted and to make progress through the political hierarchy. It is only when large numbers of women are present that existing conventions can be successfully challenged and a distinctive 'women's agenda' is able to emerge.

As with the pessimistic viewpoints, the two more positive theories are open to challenge on a number of grounds. The time-lag hypothesis assumes that women will slowly make progress irrespective of other factors, when earlier chapters of this book have already demonstrated that the rate of progress has been extremely uneven across different countries. In particular we have seen in Chapter 2 that progress was extremely limited in the first 50 years after women became politically enfranchised, and that the rate of change has increased significantly after positive action has been taken, such as the imposition of women's quotas. The critical mass theory is open to the problem that even after reaching the required proportion, women may have 'gone native' and accepted existing (male) conventions in order to make political progress. As a result of their own success, they may be unwilling to change those conventions once in a position to do so.

ARGUMENTS FOR THE PARTICIPATION OF WOMEN IN DECISION MAKING

In order to judge what difference women in power have made, it is helpful to repeat the arguments which have been put in favour of increasing the presence of women in decision-making positions. Broadly, there are three general arguments which have been advanced to support the greater participation by women in decision making: democratic justice and equity, the representation of women's interests and the efficient use of all available resources.[4] These three arguments have different implications for the question of whether women would be expected to make a clear difference in the political system. The first argument will be satisfied if women are seen to play an equal part in decision-making processes and the third will also be met if all positions are open to men and women equally. Perhaps only the second argument implies that we should expect women to make a clear difference. We shall outline each of the arguments briefly, before bringing together evidence from previous chapters and other studies to assess to what extent they have been met in western Europe in the post-war period.

Equity and democratic justice

The first argument in favour of women's full participation in the political system relates to equity and democratic justice. It is now generally accepted that there should be equality between women and men, and it follows that women should no more be excluded from politics than from any other walk of life. Indeed, one could argue that women should be entitled to at least 50 per cent representation at all levels to reflect the proportion of women in the population. It is also the case that the legitimacy of democratic political systems will be reduced if women are absent or underrepresented in key decision-making positions; public confidence in institutions may be diminished. It has even been claimed that 'there cannot be true democracy if women are excluded from positions of power'.[5]

By this argument, it is sufficient that women play a greater and ultimately equal role in decision making, even if they behave in exactly the same ways as men. It is not relevant whether women parliamentarians are seen to 'make a difference'; there is a democratic argument that women should be present in reasonable numbers. As we have seen in previous chapters, there has been a steady growth in numbers of women in the political system, though this has varied from country to country and in response to a number of other factors. As Table 8 shows, numbers of women MPs initially grew very slowly from 1945 to 1970, with the average percentage remaining well below 10 per cent.

Only since the 1970s has there been a significant increase in all countries, but even by the end of the century, the average percentage of women in national parliaments was only 25 per cent, a figure probably below the 'critical mass' which may be required for women to start to make a difference. It does appear that there has been a sharp variation between Scandinavian countries and others. In Denmark, Norway and Sweden, the number of women in parliament has been steadily rising since 1945, with the average percentage nearing the 'critical' 40 per cent by 1999. Elsewhere, progress was negligible between 1945 and 1980, and remains slow, with the average number of women in

Table 8 Percentage of women in parliament 1945–1999

	1945 %	1970 %	1980 %	1990 %	1999 %
Sweden	7.8	15.5	26.4	37.5	42.7
Denmark	5.4	10.6	23.5	29.7	37.4
Norway	4.7	9.3	23.9	35.8	36.4
Netherlands	?	8.7	14.7	23.3	36.0
Germany*	6.8	6.6	8.5	20.5	30.9
Spain	–	–	6.0	13.4	21.6
UK	3.8	4.1	3.0	6.3	18.4
Ireland	3.4	2.1	4.1	7.8	12.0
Italy	7.8	2.8	8.2	12.9	11.1
France	6.9	1.6	3.6	5.7	10.9
Average	*5.8*	*6.8*	*12.2*	*19.3*	*25.7*

Sources: E. Haavio-Mannila *et al.* (eds), *Unfinished Democracy: Women in Nordic Politics* (Oxford: Pergamon, 1985); R. Katz and P. Mair (eds), *Party Organisations. A Data Handbook* (London: Sage, 1992); J. Lovenduski and P. Norris (eds), *Gender and Party Politics* (London: Sage, 1993); S. Donnelly, *Elections '97* (Dublin: Seán Donnelly, 1998); Inter-Parliamentary Union.

Notes: Figures refer to the lower chamber of parliament only.

* The figures for Germany relate to West Germany until 1990. In that year, there were elections both in West Germany and the new unified Germany, with the proportion of women elected identical at 20.5 per cent.

non-Scandinavian countries still only at 20 per cent at the end of the century, and the figures in Ireland, Italy and France substantially lower. It is clear then that there is still some way to go in many countries before women and men are equally represented, and democracy is seen to be 'complete'.

We have argued in previous chapters that the proportion of women elected to parliament and elsewhere has varied according to a number of other factors. In Chapter 4, we suggested that women were more likely to be elected from parties of the left than parties of the right, helped by the greater willingness of the left to introduce some form of women's quotas. Chapter 5 also suggested that in general governments of the left included more women than governments of the right, and Chapter 7 noted that there had been more MEPs from parties of the left than parties of the right, though Chapter 6 did not find this pattern among local councillors. Both Chapters 4 and 6 noted that the largest proportion of women representatives at national and local levels could be found in recently formed parties such as the Greens. In Chapter 8 it was shown that women were more likely to be elected by proportional electoral systems, particularly those where a large number of representatives are elected in each constituency. And in Chapter 6 we showed that women were more likely to be elected to local government in large urban areas, such as Madrid, Stockholm and Dublin.

Representation of 'women's interests'

The second set of arguments concerns interest representation. It has been argued that men and women have different interests, and women therefore need to participate in decision-making structures for their specific interests to be articulated. By definition women's interests cannot be properly represented by men, in much the same way that it has been argued that the interests of the working class cannot fully be represented by the middle class. Incorporated within the notion of 'women's interests' may be different perspectives on issues which also matter to men. Such a 'gendered' perspective may include the bringing of different styles into the decision-making process, which will enhance its overall effectiveness. In summary, the argument is that women speak 'in a different voice', and we should therefore expect women in decision-making to change the political landscape.

It should be noted that this notion of a distinct set of 'women's interests' has been challenged by Anne Phillips, who argues that we cannot assume shared interests between women, even on issues such as abortion. The experience of being a woman may both increase the importance of legalising abortion, and make women more reluctant to have an abortion itself.[6] This makes the issue of women changing politics by 'representing women' more complex. None the less, we have already argued in Chapter 3 that women did cause changes to the formal political system 'from the outside' in the 1970s, with the development of second wave feminism and its insistence that 'the personal is political'. As a result, abortion and divorce laws were liberalised in a number of countries, and 'women's issues' such as contraception were placed firmly on the political agenda. But as women have moved into formal decision-making bodies, have they continued to make a difference or have they acted in a similar way to men?

A number of studies have now been made of women parliamentarians, with interesting results. For example, an analysis of parliamentary questions in Finland and Norway in the late 1970s discovered that women tended to take up issues dealing with 'reproduction', such as health, education and childcare, while men generally asked questions dealing with 'production' such as finance, taxation and defence.[7] And in Norway between 1973 and 1977, 20 per cent of women's interventions could be linked to 'women's interests', compared with just 4 per cent of those of men.[8] This does not necessarily prove that women in parliament see themselves as primarily representing the interests of women, but it does show that they are more likely to push agendas which are of interest to many women. However, asking questions does not itself guarantee change; women will have little control over government policy and the parliamentary agenda if they form only a small minority in leadership positions. Unfortunately, we are unaware of any studies of women in ministerial positions and the ways in which they have differed from men, possibly because their numbers have been so small.

A large study of women candidates was carried out in the 1992 British general election, which found that women were consistently more strongly in favour of women's rights, significantly more unilateralist and slightly more liberal on social issues than their male party colleagues. In addition, gender was significantly associated with the priority given to social policy issues. In terms of the 'style of politics', the British survey discovered that women gave a higher priority than men to constituency work, with a big contrast in time devoted to helping individual constituents with problems. Men spent more time in meetings and committees.[9] Such findings echo an earlier study made in the Netherlands, where female MPs judged themselves more practical, pragmatic and sensitive to their constituents than their male colleagues. They were also more inclined to compromise and to sustain contacts with MPs of other parties.[10] However, it is generally agreed that women do remain loyal to their party in parliament. Party remains a better indicator than gender on attitudes to political issues in Norway and Britain, with recent studies in Britain suggesting that women Labour MPs have been more supportive of government policies than their male counterparts since 1997. Such conformity may disappoint some, but given that women still form less than 25 per cent of the parliamentary Labour Party, it may not be too surprising given the 'critical mass' theory outlined above.

Using all available talent

The third argument in support of greater women's participation in decision making is that of resource utilisation, simply that women constitute half of the population within western Europe and elsewhere, and thus half of all potential talent and ability. The exclusion of women from the political system or any other walk of life thereby constitutes a waste of available resources, and the inclusion of women should maximise available resources and lead to improved outcomes.

As with the first argument, resource utilisation does not necessarily imply that women will change the political system, and even though one might expect the quality of policy 'outputs' to improve if women are fully involved, this may not be measurable in any meaningful sense. However, as we enter a new century, it is clear that resources are still not being maximised, and the potential talent of women is still being wasted. In particular, women remain almost totally absent from leadership positions. In Chapters 4, 5 and 6, we detailed the continued lack of women at the top of political parties, national governments, regional governments and local governments. This pattern is consistent across western Europe, even in those countries where women now make up 30 per cent or 40 per cent of parliamentary delegations. Women are not only absent from leading positions, but also from other 'high-profile' portfolios such as economics, foreign policy and defence.

Clearly, then, women's talents are still being wasted, as men continue to monopolise a number of areas. It would be hard to maintain an argument that no woman is currently capable of occupying the post of prime minister, or that so few are capable of leading finance ministries or foreign affairs ministries, or that so few are capable of leading regional councils or serving as an elected mayor of a large city. It would seem more likely that women are being held back by other factors, perhaps by continuing hostility from men, or possibly by a 'time lag' effect, since it takes even MPs a number of years before they reach the very top political posts. Whatever the reason, if greater women's representation was the challenge of the second half of the twentieth century, increasing the numbers of women in leadership positions must be the priority of the twenty-first.

Notes

1 INTRODUCTION

1 P. Graves, *Labour Women 1918–39* (Cambridge: Cambridge University Press, 1994), p. 27.
2 Quoted in G. E. Maguire, *Conservative Women* (Oxford: St Anthony's Series, 1998), p. 175.
3 M. Duverger, *The Political Role of Women* (Paris: UNESCO, 1955), p. 123.
4 K. Newland, *Women in Politics: A Global Review* (Washington: World Watch Institute), quoted in M. Stacey and M. Price, *Women, Power and Politics* (London: Tavistock, 1981), p. 133.
5 M. Kelber, *Women and Government: New Ways to Political Power* (New York: Praeger, 1994), p. 93.
6 J. Bussemaker and R. Voet, *Gender, Participation and Citizenship in the Netherlands* (Aldershot: Ashgate, 1998), p. 51.
7 M. Stacey and M. Price, *Women, Power and Politics* (London: Tavistock, 1981), p. 7.
8 European Commission: Employment and Social Affairs Directorate, *Equal Opportunities for Women and Men in the European Union: Annual Report 1998*, pp. 17, 49.
9 European Commission: Employment and Social Affairs Directorate, *Women in Decision-making* (Brussels, 1999), p. 3.
10 One significant exception is the study by Hege Skjeie of the political integration of women in Norway, using analyses of party documents together with in-depth interviews of women and men politicians. See H. Skjeie, 'Ending the Male Political Hegemony: The Norwegian Experience', in J. Lovenduski and P. Norris (eds), *Gender and Party Politics* (London: Sage, 1993).

2 SLOW PROGRESS, 1945–1970

1 See, for example, D. Simonton, *A History of European Women's Work* (London: Routledge, 1998), pp. 185–7; G. Braybon and P. Summerfield, *Out of the Cage: Women's Experiences in Two World Wards* (London: Routledge, 1987); R. Mackay, *The Test of War: Inside Britain 1939–45* (London: UCL Press, 1999), pp. 220–6.

2 A. Owings, *Frauen* (Harmondsworth: Penguin, 1993); C. Koonz, *Mothers in the Fatherland* (London: Methuen, 1988).
3 Quoted in Mackay, op. cit., p. 227.
4 Ibid., p. 225.
5 Ibid., pp. 77–80.
6 E. Kolinsky, *Women in Contemporary Germany* (Oxford: Berg, 1993), pp. 33–4.
7 M. Pugh, *Women and the Women's Movement in Britain, 1914–1959* (Basingstoke: Macmillan, 1992), p. 289.
8 Kolinsky, op. cit., p. 37.
9 P. Graves, *Labour Women 1918–39* (Cambridge: Cambridge University Press, 1994), p. 220.
10 E. Mahon, 'Women's Rights and Catholicism in Ireland', in M. Threlfall (ed.), *Mapping the Women's Movement* (London: Verso, 1996), p. 187.
11 J. Lovenduski and J. Hills, *The Politics of the Second Electorate* (London: Routledge & Kegan Paul, 1981), p. 159.
12 Graves, op. cit.; J. Liddington, *The Long Road to Greenham* (London: Virago, 1989).
13 J. Bystydzienski, *Women Transforming Politics* (Bloomington: Indiana University Press, 1992), pp. 15–16.
14 S. Reynolds, *France Between the Wars* (London: Routledge, 1996), p. 219.
15 M. Duverger, *The Political Role of Women* (Paris: UNESCO, 1955), pp. 162–6.
16 Kolinsky, op. cit., p. 197.
17 Bystydzienski, op. cit., p. 159.
18 Ibid., p. 190.
19 Kolinsky, op. cit., pp. 200–1.
20 J. Lovenduski and P. Norris, *Gender and Party Politics* (London: Sage, 1993), p. 38.
21 P. Brookes, *Women at Westminster* (London: Peter Davies, 1967), p. 177.
22 Ibid., p. 239.
23 M. Thatcher, *The Path to Power* (London: HarperCollins, 1995), p. 28.
24 P. Hollis, *Jennie Lee: A Life* (Oxford: Oxford University Press, 1997), pp. 7–8.
25 J. Bussemaker and R. Voet, *Gender, Participation and Citizenship in the Netherlands* (Aldershot: Ashgate, 1998), p. 96.
26 Ibid., p. 95.
27 Thatcher, op. cit., p. 94.
28 Brookes, op. cit., p. 229.
29 Ibid., p. 150.
30 Thatcher, op. cit., p. 108; E. Summerskill, *A Woman's World* (London: Heinemann, 1967), p. 61.
31 Pugh, op. cit., p. 277.
32 Hollis, op. cit., p. 150.
33 Thatcher, op. cit., p. 144. Thatcher's memoirs need to be treated with particular care, as they invariably portray their subject in a very favourable light, while disparaging political opponents such as Edward Heath.
34 M. Kelber (ed.), *Women and Government: New Ways to Political Power* (New York: Praeger, 1994), p. 99.

3 SECOND WAVE FEMINISM: THE 1970s AND EARLY 1980s

1 'First wave feminism' is used to describe the many campaigns for female suffrage waged by women between the late nineteenth century and 1945. See V. Randall, *Women and Politics: An International Perspective* (Basingstoke: Macmillan, 1982), pp. 208–18.
2 For the impact in 1963 of Betty Frieden's book *The Feminine Mystique* (first published London: Victor Gollancz, 1963; Penguin, 1965) and the creation in the USA of the National Organisation of Women in 1966 see Randall, op. cit., pp. 224–5.
3 D. Dahlerup (ed.), *The New Women's Movement* (London: Sage, 1986), p. 1.
4 J. Lovenduski and J. Hills (eds), *The Politics of the Second Electorate* (London: Routledge & Kegan Paul, 1981), p. 6.
5 Dahlerup, op. cit., pp. 93, 217.
6 C. T. Adams and C. T. Winston, *Mothers at Work* (London: Longman, 1980), p. 139.
7 M. Kelber, *Women and Government: New Ways to Political Power* (New York: Praeger, 1994), p. 101.
8 J. Lovenduski, *Women and European Politics: Contemporary Feminism and Public Policy* (Boston: Massachusetts University Press, 1986), p. 277.
9 Ibid., p. 12.
10 Ibid., p. 17.
11 Dahlerup, op. cit., p. 226.
12 Kelber, op. cit., pp. 141–2.
13 Ibid., p. 141.
14 Dahlerup, op. cit., pp. 241–2.
15 M. F. Katzenstein and C. Mueller (eds), *The Women's Movements of the United States and Western Europe* (Philadelphia: Temple University Press, 1987), p. 46.
16 Dahlerup, op. cit., p. 64.
17 Lovenduski, op. cit., p. 276.
18 J. Jenson, 'Representations of Difference: Varieties of French Feminism', in M. Threlfall (ed.), *Mapping the Women's Movement* (London: Verso, 1996), pp. 73–108.
19 Lovenduski, op. cit., p. 95.
20 Dahlerup, op. cit., p. 95.
21 Randall, op. cit., p. 246.
22 Dahlerup, op. cit., p. 99.
23 Ibid., p. 29.
24 Katzenstein and Mueller, op. cit., p. 135.
25 Lovenduski and Hills, op. cit., p. 200.
26 Quoted in Randall, op. cit., p. 238.
27 Dahlerup, op. cit., p. 35.
28 Ibid., p. 34.
29 Ibid., p. 205.
30 Ibid., p. 109.
31 In 1975, James White's Private Member's Bill to restrict the 1967 Abortion Act got as far as a second reading, and in 1979 John Corrie drew first place in the ballot for private members' bills, and tried again, unsuccessfully, to get a bill restricting abortion onto the statute book. Eighty thousand

people joined in a march organised by the trade union movement, with input from women's groups, to express their opposition to the measure.
32 Lovenduski, op. cit., p. 78.
33 Quoted in J. Liddington, *The Long Road to Greenham* (London: Virago, 1989), p. 174.
34 Randall, op. cit., p. 77.
35 Liddington, op. cit., p. 254.
36 S. Parkin, *The Life and Death of Petra Kelly* (London: Pandora, 1995), pp. 70–1.

4 WOMEN IN POLITICAL PARTIES

1 For example, the Dutch Protestant Party did not allow women to stand for election until 1953.
2 E. Kolinsky, *Women in Contemporary Germany* (Oxford: Berg, 1993), pp. 209–10.
3 E. Haavio-Mannila *et al.* (eds), *Unfinished Democracy: Women in Nordic Politics* (Oxford: Pergamon, 1985), pp. 46–7. The most successful example of a women's party in the post-war period has been in Iceland, where in 1983 three representatives were elected to the national parliament on a 5.5 per cent share of the vote.
4 L. Mayer and R. Smith, 'Feminism and Religiosity: Female Electoral Behaviour in Western Europe', in S. Bashevkin (ed.), *Women and Politics in Western Europe* (London: Frank Cass, 1985), p. 42.
5 J. Bussemaker and R. Voet, *Gender, Participation and Citizenship in the Netherlands* (Aldershot: Ashgate, 1998), p. 97.
6 D. Sainsbury, 'The Politics of Increased Women's Representation: The Swedish Case', in J. Lovenduski and P. Norris (eds), *Gender and Party Politics* (London: Sage, 1993), pp. 280–1.
7 S. Perrigo, 'Women and Change in the Labour Party 1979–1995', in J. Lovenduski and P. Norris (eds), *Women in Politics* (Oxford: Oxford University Press, 1996), p. 121.
8 E. Kolinsky, 'Party Change and Women's Representation in Unified Germany', in J. Lovenduski and P. Norris (eds), *Gender and Party Politics*, p. 128.
9 P. Graves, *Labour Women 1918–39* (Cambridge: Cambridge University Press, 1994), p. 29.
10 Kolinsky, op. cit., p. 5.
11 M. Kelber, *Women and Government* (New York: Praeger, 1994), pp. 66–7; J. Bystydzienski, 'Norway', in W. Rule and J. Zimmerman (eds), *Electoral Systems in Comparative Perspective: Their Impact on Women and Minorities* (Westport: Greenwood, 1994), pp. 59–61.
12 M. Thatcher, *The Path to Power* (London: HarperCollins, 1995), p. 94.
13 C. Short 'Women in the Labour Party', in J. Lovenduski and P. Norris (eds), *Women in Politics* (Oxford: Oxford University Press, 1996), p. 23.
14 Sainsbury, op. cit.
15 See J. Lovenduski and P. Norris (eds), *Gender and Party Politics* (Sage, 1993); Haavio-Mannila *et al.*, op. cit., pp. 44–5.
16 Lovenduski and Norris (eds), *Gender and Party Politics*, pp. 40–4.

17 Short, op. cit.
18 A. Appleton and A. Mazur, 'Transformation or Modernization: the Rhetoric and Reality of Gender and Party Politics in France', in J. Lovenduski and P. Norris (eds), *Gender and Party Politics*, p. 103.
19 W. Northcutt and J. Flaitz, 'Women, Politics and the French Socialist Government', in S. Bashevkin (ed.), *Women and Politics in Western Europe* (London: Frank Cass, 1985), p. 55.
20 M. Guadagnini, 'A Partitocrazia Without Women: The Case of the Italian Party System', in J. Lovenduski and P. Norris, *Women in Politics*.
21 EU Committee of the Regions, *Regional and Local Democracy in the European Union* (EU, 1999), p. 159.
22 E. Vallance, 'Women Candidates in the 1983 General Election' (*Parliamentary Affairs*, vol. 37, 1984).
23 J. Squires, 'Quotas for Women: Fair Representation?' in Lovenduski and Norris, *Women in Politics*, p. 75.

5 WOMEN IN GOVERNMENT

1 D. Wilsford, (ed.), *Political Leaders of Contemporary Western Europe* (Westport: Greenwood Press, 1995).
2 C. Ysmal, 'France', in R. Katz and R. Koole (eds), *Political Data Yearbook 1998* (*European Journal of Political Research*, vol. 34, nos. 3–4), pp. 397–8.
3 M. Duverger, *The Political Role of Women* (Paris: UNESCO, 1955).
4 M. Genovese, *Women as National Leaders* (London: Sage, 1993), p. 222.
5 W. Northcutt and J. Flaitz, 'Women, Politics and the French Socialist Government', in Bashevkin, S. (ed.), *Women and Politics in Western Europe* (London: Frank Cass, 1985), p. 58.
6 Ibid., p. 59.
7 M. Threlfall, *Mapping the Women's Movement* (London: Verso, 1996), pp. 124–5.
8 Y. Galligan, *Women and Politics in Contemporary Ireland* (London: Pinter, 1998), p. 62.
9 Lady Jay was Minister for Women in 1999, but was also responsible for reforming the House of Lords.
10 M. Kelber, *Women and Government: New Ways to Political Power* (New York: Praeger, 1994), p. 69.
11 M. Leijenaar, 'Political Empowerment of Women in the Netherlands', in J. Bussemaker and R. Voet (eds), *Gender, Participation and Citizenship in the Netherlands* (Aldershot: Ashgate, 1998).

6 WOMEN IN LOCAL GOVERNMENT

1 Figures taken from the Council of European Municipalities and Regions study, *Women in Local Politics in the European Union* (CEMR, Oct. 1999) and European Parliament Directorate for Research, *Differential Impact of Electoral Systems on Female Political Representation* (Women's Right Series, no. 8, Brussels, 1997).

2 C. Rallings and M. Thrasher, *Local Elections in Britain* (London: Routledge, 1997), pp. 76–8.
3 European Parliament Directorate for Research, op. cit., chapter 4.
4 Study by Marila Guadagnini (1987) quoted in European Commission, Employment and Social Affairs Directorate, *Women in Decision Making* (Brussels, 1999), p. 13; Rallings and Thrasher, op. cit., pp. 69–79.
5 P. Dini, *Women's Participation in Political Life in the Regions of Europe* (Congress of Local and Regional Authorities of Europe, Chamber of Regions, Sixth Session, 15–17 June 1999), p. 20.
6 European Network of Experts, *Panorama: Participation of Women in Political Decision-making at Regional and Local Level* (European Commission, Brussels, 1994), pp. 20, 27.
7 Rallings and Thrasher, op. cit., pp. 71–2.
8 E. Kolinsky, 'Party Change and Women's Representation in Unified Germany', in J. Lovenduski and P. Norris, *Gender and Party Politics* (London: Sage, 1993), p. 139.
9 P. Brookes, *Women at Westminster* (London: Peter Davies, 1967), p. 239.
10 P. Graves, *Labour Women 1918–39* (Cambridge: Cambridge University Press, 1994), p. 176.
11 European Commission report, ed. J. Lovanduski and S. Stephenson, *Women in Decision-making: Report on Existing Research in the European Union* (Belgium, 1999), pp. 9–10, 12.
12 European Network of Experts, op. cit., pp. 17, 25.
13 CEMR, *Women in Local Politics in the European Union*, figures for the UK (Brussels, October 1999).
14 M. Leijenaar, *How to Create a Gender Balance in Political Decision-making* (European Commission, Employment and Social Affairs, Brussels, 1996), p. 20; L. Corral Ruiz, 'The Role of Women in Local Government', in CEMTR, *Men and Women in European Municipalities* (Paris: CEMR, 1998), p. 24.
15 E. Elgan, 'Advantages and Obstacles: The Swedish Experience', in CEMTR, *Men and Women in European Municipalities*, pp. 44–5.
16 Dini, op. cit., p. 34.
17 European Network of Experts, op. cit., p. 44.
18 J. Bussemaker and R. Voet, *Gender, Participation and Citizenship in the Netherlands* (Aldershot: Ashgate, 1998), p. 100.
19 F. Gaspard, 'Women Elected Representatives in French Municipalities', in CEMR, *Men and Women in European Municipalities*, pp. 38–9.
20 M. Ruggerini, 'The Presence of Women in Italian Politics', in CEMR, *Men and Women in European Municipalities*, p. 61; Gaspard, op. cit., p. 41.
21 R. Henig, 'Women and Political Power in the 1990s', in T. Cosslett, A. Easton and P. Summerfield (eds), 'Women, Power and Resistance (Buckingham: Open University Press, 1996), pp. 268–9.
22 European Network of Exports, op. cit., pp. 52–7.
23 Committee of the Regions, *Regional and Local Democracy in the European Union* (Brussels, May 1999), p. 52.
24 Leijenaar, op. cit., p. 15.

7 THE INTERNATIONAL CONTEXT: IMPACT OF THE EUROPEAN UNION AND UNITED NATIONS

1 European Commission, Employment and Social Affairs Directorate, *Equal Opportunities for Women and Men in the European Union*, Annual Reports for 1996, 1997, 1998.
2 European Commission, Employment and Social Affairs Directorate, *Equal Opportunities*, Annual Report for 1997, p. 98.
3 J. Lovenduski, *Women and European Politics: Contemporary Feminism and Public Policy* (Brighton: Wheatsheaf, 1986), pp. 162–3.
4 European Commission, Employment and Social Affairs Directorate, *Equal Opportunities*, Annual Report 1996, pp. 8, 16.
5 European Commission, Employment and Social Affairs Directorate, *Third Medium-term Action Programme on Equal Opportunities for Women and Men*: Commission Staff working paper, p. iv.
6 European Commission, *Women of Europe* newsletter, May/June 1999.
7 European Commission, Employment and Social Affairs Directorate, *Equal Opportunities*, Annual Report 1996, pp. 85–91.
8 European Commission, Employment and Social Affairs Directorate, *Equal Opportunities*, Annual Report 1997, p. 99.
9 Ibid., pp. 101–2.
10 European Commission, Employment and Social Affairs Directorate, *Equal Opportunities*, Annual Report 1998, pp. 86–7.
11 European Commission, *Women in Europe* newsletter, Sept. 1999, no. 88.
12 European Commission, Employment and Social Affairs Directorate, *Equal Opportunities*, Annual Report 1998, p. 21.
13 European Parliament, *The Work of the Committee on Women's Rights 1994–9*, Women's Rights Series, FEMM 105 EN.
14 See, for example, CLRAE, Sixth Session, Strasbourg June 1999, *Women's Participation in Political Life in the Regions of Europe* (Rapporteur Ms Dini) and CEMR, *Men and Women in European Municipalities*, June 1998.
15 European Commission, Employment and Social Affairs Directorate, *Equal Opportunities*, Annual Report 1998, p. 89.
16 European Commission, Employment and Social Affairs Directorate, *Equal Opportunities*, Annual Report 1996, pp. 116–20.
17 European Commission, *Women of Europe* newsletter, May/June 1999.

8 ELECTORAL SYSTEMS

1 P. Norris, 'Women's Legislative Participation in Western Europe', in S. Bashevkin (ed.), *Women and Politics in Western Europe* (London: Frank Cass, 1985).
2 W. Rule and J. Zimmerman, *Electoral Systems in Comparative Perspective: Their Impact on Women and Minorities* (Westport: Greenwood Press, 1994), p. 16.
3 A number of two-member constituencies also existed for parliamentary elections before the war.

4 France used a proportional system for parliamentary elections before 1958 and again briefly in 1986.
5 The single transferable vote also allows the voter to list preferences up to the number of candidates on the ballot paper. Candidates are elected when they exceed the 'quota' which is the total number of votes cast divided by the number of seats plus one. Excess votes are redistributed to the second preference, and candidates are also eliminated from the bottom until all seats are filled.
6 Rule and Zimmerman, op. cit., p. 18.
7 D. Leonard and R. Natkiel, *World Atlas of Elections* (London: Economist Publications, 1986).
8 J. Bystydzienski, 'Norway', in Rule and Zimmerman, op. cit., p. 57.
9 E. Kolinsky, 'Party Change and Women's Representation in Unified Germany', in J. Lovenduski and P. Norris (eds), *Gender and Party Politics* (London: Sage), p. 141–2.
10 J. Jenson, 'Representations of Difference: The Varieties of French Feminism', in M. Threlfall (ed.), *Mapping the Women's Movement* (London: Verso, 1996), p. 105.
11 M. Guadagnini, 'A *Partitocrazia* Without Women: the Case of the Italian Party System', in J. Lovenduski and P. Norris (eds), *Gender and Party Politics* (London: Sage, 1993), p. 185.
12 N. Raaum, 'The Political Representation of Women: A Bird's Eye View', in L. Karvonen and P. Selle (eds), *Women in Nordic Politics: Closing the Gap* (London: Dartmouth, 1995), p. 36.

9 CONCLUSION: DO WOMEN MAKE A DIFFERENCE?

1 A. D. Christensen and P. K. Damkjoer, 'Women and Political Representation in Denmark' (Aalborg: Aalborg University working paper, 1998).
2 See N. Raaum, 'The Political Representation of Women: A Bird's Eye View', in L. Karvonen and P. Selle (eds), *Women in Nordic Politics: Closing the Gap* (London: Dartmouth, 1995).
3 D. Dahlerup, 'From a Small to a Large Minority. Women in Scandinavian Politics' (*Scandinavian Political Studies*, no. 2, 1988), pp. 275–98.
4 See for example I. Norderval, 'Party and Legislative Participation among Scandinavian Women', in S. Bashevkin (ed.), *Women and Politics in Western Europe* (London: Frank Cass, 1985), p. 84; P. Norris, 'Women Politicians: Transforming Westminster?' in J. Lovenduski and P. Norris (eds), *Women in Politics* (Oxford: Oxford University Press, 1996), pp. 91–2; and M. Leijenaar, *How to Create a Gender Balance in Political Decisionmaking* (European Commission, 1996).
5 Leijenaar, op. cit., p. 13.
6 A. Phillips, *Engendering Democracy* (London: Polity, 1981), pp. 72–3.
7 E. Haavio-Mannila *et al.* (eds), *Unfinished Democracy: Women in Nordic Politics* (Oxford: Pergamon, 1985), pp. 74–5.
8 Norderval, op. cit., p. 85.
9 Norris, op. cit.
10 B. Nelson and N. Chowdhury (eds), *Women and Politics Worldwide* (New Haven: Yale University Press, 1994), p. 504.

Guide to further reading

BOOKS

Bashevkin, S. (ed.) (1985) *Women and Politics in Western Europe* (London: Frank Cass). Interesting collection of papers on a range of topics.

Brill, A. (ed.) (1995) *A Rising Public Voice: Women in Politics Worldwide* (New York: The Feminist Press at the City University of New York). Compilation of articles and brief biographies of women from across the world.

Brookes, P. (1967) *Women at Westminster* (London: Peter Davies). The experiences of British women MPs from 1918 up to 1966.

Bussemaker, J. and Voet, R. (1998) *Gender Participation and Citizenship in the Netherlands* (Aldershot: Ashgate). Detailed study of gender issues in the Netherlands.

Bystydzienski, J. (ed.) (1992) *Women Transforming Politics* (Bloomington: Indiana University Press). Looks at the importance of women's involvement in decision making and moves on to a number of case studies, including Norway and Spain.

Dahlerup, D. (ed.) (1986) *The New Women's Movement* (London: Sage). Series of chapters detailing the rise of the women's movement across a number of countries.

Duverger, M. (1955) *The Political Role of Women* (Paris: UNESCO). Classic early study of women's attitudes and their absence from the political system.

Galligan, Y. (1998) *Women and Politics in Contemporary Ireland* (London: Pinter). Useful book outlining the progress of women in the Republic of Ireland.

Graves, P. (1994) *Labour Women 1918–39* (Cambridge: Cambridge University Press). Interesting and detailed study of the experiences of British working-class women in the inter-war period, both within the Labour Party and in wider political activity.

Haavio-Mannila, E. *et al.* (eds) (1985) *Unfinished Democracy: Women in Nordic Politics* (Oxford: Pergamon). Detailed study of women in the political system in Scandinavia.

Karvonen, L. and Selle, P. (1995) *Women in Nordic Politics: Closing the Gap* (Aldershot: Dartmouth). Range of well-written chapters on the progress of women in Scandinavia.

Katzenstein, M. F. and Mueller, C. (1987) *The Women's Movements of the United States and Western Europe* (Philadelphia: Temple University Press). Some interesting detailed material on women's movements, particularly Italy and the Netherlands.

Kelber, M. (1994) *Women and Government: New Ways to Political Power* (New York: Praeger). Useful summary of women's progress in Scandinavia and Germany.

Kolinsky, E. (1993) *Women in Contemporary Germany* (Oxford: Berg). Detailed study of women's progress in politics, employment and education since 1945.

Liddington, J. (1989) *The Long Road to Greenham* (London: Virago). Looks at the involvement of women in the British peace movement in the twentieth century, in particular the establishment of the women's peace camp at Greenham Common.

Lovenduski, J. (1986) *Women and European Politics: Contemporary Feminism and Public Policy* (Boston: Massachusetts University Press). Looks in detail at the problems faced by women in a number of European countries and the progress made up to the mid-1980s in addressing them.

Lovenduski, J. and Hills, J. (eds) (1981) *The Politics of the Second Electorate* (London: Routledge & Kegan Paul). Useful collection of chapters on progress up to 1980 in a number of countries.

Lovenduski, J. and Norris, P. (eds) (1993) *Gender and Party Politics* (London: Sage). Detailed studies of women in political parties in western Europe and beyond.

Lovenduski, J. and Norris, P. (eds) (1996) *Women in Politics* (Oxford: Oxford University Press). Collection of chapters and articles on women in British politics.

Maguire, G. E. (1998) *Conservative Women* (Oxford: St Anthony's Series). A useful survey on an area not covered extensively elsewhere.

Nelson, B. and Chowdhury, N. (eds) (1994) *Women and Politics Worldwide* (New Haven: Yale University Press). Vast compilation volume on the political participation of women in 43 countries across the world.

Phillips, A. (1991) *Engendering Democracy* (Cambridge: Polity Press). An examination of liberal democracy from a feminist perspective.

Pugh, M. (1992) *Women and the Women's Movement in Britain 1914– 1959* (Basingstoke: Macmillan). Interesting study of the political progress of women in Britain from enfranchisement to just after the Second World War.

Randall, V. (1982) *Women and Politics: An International Perspective* (Basingstoke: Macmillan). Useful summary of the women's movement in the United States, Britain and elsewhere.

Rule, W. and Zimmerman, J. (eds) (1994) *Electoral Systems in Comparative Perspective: Their Impact on Women and Minorities* (Westport: Greenwood Press). Includes an overall assessment of the effect of electoral systems and chapters on individual countries.

Stacey, M. and Price, M. (1981) *Women, Power and Politics* (London: Tavistock). A wide-ranging survey of the problems faced by women in Britain in social, economic and political fields up to the end of the 1970s.

Threlfall, M. (ed.) (1996) *Mapping the Women's Movement* (London: Verso). Compilation of chapters covering the rise of the women's movement in countries in Europe and elsewhere.

EUROPEAN UNION PUBLICATIONS

Council of European Municipalities and Regions (CEMR) (1998) *Men and Women in European Municipalities Assessment* (Paris: CEMR). Useful summary of women in local government in Europe.

Commission of the European Communities (1996–9) *Equal Opportunities for Women and Men in the European Union: Annual Reports* (European Commission: Employment and Social Affairs). Series which began in 1996, giving useful data on women in decision making and other areas.

European Network of Experts 'Women in Decision-making' (1994) *Panorama: Participation of Women in Political Decision-making at Regional and Local Level* (European Commission). Summary of political systems, women's representation and strategies to promote women.

Leijenaar, M. (1997) *How to Create a Gender Balance in Political Decision-making* (European Commission: Employment and Social Affairs). Examines the underrepresentation of women and actions taken to redress the balance.

Lovenduski, J. and Stephenson, S. (1998) *Women in Decision-making: Report on Existing Research in the European Union* (European Commission: Employment and Social Affairs). Includes country-by-country bibliographies.

USEFUL WEB ADDRESSES

European Database: Women in Decision-making *http://www.db-decision.de/english/*. Provides access to a huge database on women in decision making in all western European countries, including women leaders and women in parliament.

International IDEA: Women in Politics *http://www.int-idea.se/women/index.htm*. Provides a range of useful information.

Inter-Parliamentary Union *http://www.ipu.org/*. Regularly updates the proportions of women in national parliaments across the world. Also provides access to a database on each country, including electoral systems and recent elections.

Index